Acclaim for *Live Compassion*

"In the gentle embrace of this profound guidebook, Kathy's insightfulness, clarity, and skill as a compassionate teacher resonate deeply. Each page exudes wisdom and practical guidance that supports the reader in transformation and the integration of Nonviolent Communication (NVC). A beautiful testament to the power of compassion, this book invites readers to delve into the heart of NVC, where self-awareness and authentic connections flourish."

—Sarah Peyton,
Author of *Your Resonant Self, Your Resonant Self Workbook,*
and co-author of *The Antiracist Heart.*

"*Live Compassion* is much more than a guidebook for living with nonviolence and empathy. It's a loving, empathetic companion for the difficult process of becoming a better human. Kathy's work is a soul-satisfying gift, especially for those who struggle--which is all of us."

—Jerry Colonna,
author of *Reboot: Leadership and the Art of Growing Up*
and *Reunion: Leadership and the Longing to Belong.*

"A treasure chest of comforting and compelling wisdom! *Live Compassion* makes the Nonviolent Communication process come alive and brings life-changing learning into daily focus. Healing happens in self-connection, and meaningful connection with others grows as you follow Kathy's journey in poetry and prose. More than a daily guidebook, it is a treasure map to dive into our journeys and harvest our hearts' gems. It is a true celebration of an NVC way of living."

—**Marie R Miyashiro,**
Author of *The Empathy Factor* and Co-author with Marshall Rosenberg of the Integrated Clarity® Chapter in the *The Change Handbook -Today's Best Methods for Engaging Whole Systems.*

"Explore the practices contained within the pages of *Live Compassion,* and you will find that this guidebook is about so much more than communication: It is about transformation. With concise clarity, author Kathy Ziola invites you to explore the depths of Nonviolent Communication as she compassionately guides you into deeper connections that may transform your relationship with yourself, others, and your world. Enjoy the journey!"

—**Rev. David Howard,**
author of *In This Moment,* inspirational musician, and co-founder of The Center for Life Enrichment.

"The world's great spiritual traditions teach that all life, all creation, is an expression of one divine love. The sage Ramana Maharshi was once asked, "How should we treat others?" He responded, "There are no others." Judeo-Christian belief systems are predicated on the notion of loving God and loving thy neighbor as thyself because your neighbor and the divine aren't separate. If we aspire to embody these enlightened teachings, what are the implications for our use of language and the way we think about and interact with others? Non-Violent

Communication (NVC) provides a simple, sophisticated way to reframe our language and interactions to embody this noble ideal of compassionate consciousness. It is simple and sophisticated but takes work to apply. Kathy Ziola makes it as easy as possible, so much so that even if you believe we are separate, competitive entities in a cold, cruel world, the wisdom in this book will help you get along better with everyone. She offers a wise, creative, practical guide to connecting with ourselves, preventing and healing conflict, and making life more beautiful. Highly recommended!"

—**Michael J. Gelb,**
author of *How to Think Like Leonardo da Vinci*
and *The Art of Connection.*

"Kathy Ziola sets an ambitious goal in her book, *Live Compassion, Your Daily Guidebook for Integrating Nonviolent Communication.* She seeks to guide us on a daily experience with compassion – first with the self, and then with the other. As she sets out the key assumptions, principles, and components of Nonviolent Communication (NVC), she is direct and easy to follow. She is so direct, in fact, she offers 365 daily practices to deepen our insight into the benefits and empathic power of NVC. Though it gives an appropriate nod to the work of Marshall Rosenberg, the founder of NVC, this book does not engage in a theoretical analysis of his work. Instead, it's rich with personal insight and grounded advice. Each day you get a new angle to consider, a new practice to follow, or a new focus to apply to your communication and listening needs. You learn how to listen to yourself. You learn how to listen to others. It's an easy read. And anyone interested in the exploration of the self should read it."

—**Bobby DiCello,**
Nationally Recognized Trial Lawyer and
Television Commentator

Live Compassion

YOUR DAILY GUIDEBOOK FOR INTEGRATING NONVIOLENT COMMUNICATION

KATHY ZIOLA, MA

Feast Publishing

For information about special discounts for bulk purchases, please contact kathy@nvctrainingsource.com or call 970-216-8597

Cover and interior design by Quantum Shift Media

ISBN: 978-0-9826130-2-3 Print
ISBN: 978-0-9826130-3-0 eBook
Library of Congress: LCCN 2023915126

Printed in the United States of America

Feast Publishing
Loveland, Colorado

Table of Contents

Dedication

I dedicate this book to the many NVC students I have worked with who asked for more support, daily reminders, and ways to keep NVC top of mind.

To you, my readers, longing to live from your heart of love and compassion.

To everyone who passionately wants to communicate with authenticity and empathy.

To all of us whose deepest heart desire is to be fully ourselves, expressing our truth with kindness and consideration for each other, ourselves, and the world.

May this guidebook be a joy to you in manifesting these beautiful desires.

Acknowledgments

My deepest gratitude to Marshall Rosenberg, PhD, the founder of Nonviolent Communication (NVC), for giving the world this powerful gift of relating from a heart of compassion.

Appreciation for my mentors in NVC who taught, supported, and guided me as I began this journey: Miki Kashtan, Robert Gonzales, Wes Taylor, Susan Skye, Penny Wassman, Inbal Kashtan, and Francois Beausolais. These dear ones have inspired me and been role models for me.

And heartfelt appreciation to Neelam for years of deep inquiry work, emotional support, and work in Presence, which is a foundational part of my ability to work with people today in all my capacities.

Introduction

I Journeyed Here

I was on a getaway with friends in Taos, New Mexico when one friend handed me the book *Nonviolent Communication* by Marshall B. Rosenberg, PhD. As a longtime personal growth participant with a history of organizing and leading relationship training events and a huge passion for great communication, I said, "That looks interesting. I'll have to read it sometime."

Four months later a friend called and invited me to attend a workshop in Nonviolent Communication she was organizing. I offered to help organize that event, and halfway through the training, I was online looking for the next learning opportunity. I knew I had found something powerful and wanted to learn and teach it. Two weeks later, I was at a five-day retreat deepening my learning. I was in intensive training for the next four years.

For me, NVC was the missing link. I was a therapist already, with years of meditation, personal development, and a deep passion for waking up and living in love. I had a lot of tools already, but something was missing. For me, NVC was the missing link, the link between ideals and values and *how* to bring them into daily living and interaction. Have you ever had the experience of sitting on the meditation pillow or in a great church service and finding deep peace and joy, and then walking out to the kitchen or living room or going home from church and suddenly finding yourself reactive and upset with someone? This is a story I experienced and heard from many people struggling for congruence between core values and how to live them. NVC provides a strategy to meet that longing. It is like a toolbox filled with tools for building the consciousness and skills to connect compassionately with our inner experience and communicate in ways that connect deeply, respectfully, and kindly with others.

I practiced every day, doing worksheets, trying out NVC in any interaction I could, from the bookstore clerk to my long-distance relationships, sharing it with my young kids, and using it as an owner of a wellness collective with twelve other people. Every area of life I could think of was fair game. There are endless opportunities for practicing better communication! I learned a ton by teaching. Since 2005, I have taught in a variety of settings from classes for the public, to luxury hotel staff, county human services department, schools, a hospital oncology department, and a county parks and open space department, just to name a few.

Through the years of living and sharing NVC, I have continued to practice daily to be mindful, use the tools, and connect more deeply. I have less reactivity, more equanimity, and a clear path to expressing myself well, understanding deeply, and offering empathy. This gives me confidence as I meet the challenging conversations life inevitably brings.

Inspiration for This Book

Think about the first or second language that you or your child learned. You or they started out making the sounds of syllables and then putting them together into words and words into phrases, phrases into sentences, sentences into stories and conversations. This took time and a lot of practice! This took encouragement and feedback. It required attention every single day for several years!

Learning a new way of speaking and thinking is much like the experience of learning that first language. Reading a book, watching a video, or taking a class is a great start. And it also takes practice and attention to learn and integrate new habits and perspectives. This book will help you do just that.

> "I wish I could carry you around on my shoulder to whisper in my ear."
>
> "I have a hard time remembering to use my NVC in day-to-day life."
>
> "I need help with something to focus on each day to keep me on track."
>
> "When I'm in a tough conversation, I often ask myself, 'What would Kathy say or do now?'"
>
> These remarks from training participants inspired me to put this exploration guide together to support you in daily awareness and practice of NVC.

The 365 explorations in this book have come from my years of teaching NVC. They have been inspired by my challenges and applications of the work and by the questions of the many students I have worked with over the years. They were inspired by moments of beauty and pain that coaching clients have met and moved through and the practices that arose in me to offer in response to those challenges. They were inspired by the direct experience of doing each of these things over the years and finding that the practices gave me ever-expanding self-awareness, curiosity, and integration. These practices have been part of my personal journey of waking up to my deeper self and living my values with more and more congruence and compassion for myself and others. It is my heartfelt desire that they will serve you in similar ways.

This book provides inspiration, ideas, and practices to support you in integrating and living the principles and using the skills of NVC, also known as Compassionate Communication. The introduction to the model that follows will help you use this guide whether NVC is new to you or you have taken a class and are looking for daily guidance.

I invite you to take a course with me as soon as possible. You can find courses on my website at www.nvctrainingsource.com. I also suggest reading the book "Nonviolent Communication, A Language of Life" by Marshall B. Rosenberg, PhD. These two strategies will give you a more in-depth foundation to work with as you move through this workbook and daily exploration guide.

Nonviolent Communication Basics

"What I want in my life is compassion, a flow between myself and others based on a mutual giving from the heart." (Marshall B. Rosenberg, Nonviolent Communication, A Language of Life, PuddledancerPress, 2003 p. 1.)

I am sharing a few of the NVC basics with you as a starting point. This is a quick overview just so you have a sense of what we are working with.

Intentions of NVC

People from all walks of life struggle with relationships, whether it's with friends, family, coworkers, or romantic partners. Relationships are based on communication. Communication is a skill that, for most of us, was unconsciously gained through modeling and by trial and error. I have found that what we have in common is a lot of pain from unmet needs in relating that very often stem from communication challenges and misunderstandings of human behavior and intentions. NVC offers a very practical approach to developing communication habits that meet more needs, more consistently than the happenstance training we may have received growing up.

NVC intends to create a quality of understanding and connection where there is a sense of compassion, and everyone's needs matter. It intends to inspire people to give and receive from the heart. People working together to meet needs peacefully is highly valued in NVC. Having relationships based on authenticity and empathy is the main goal. (Marshall B. Rosenberg, *Nonviolent Communication, A Language of Life*, Puddledancer press, 2003)

Key Assumptions of the Model

The following are basic premises of NVC. I invite you to adopt them as you work with this model. See how they affect you and your interactions and whether holding them serves you to better understand yourself and others. Ask yourself whether they help you experience more connection and compassion.

1. Human needs are universal. NVC holds that there are needs and values that most human beings can relate to and appreciate, even though we may hold them in different priority status. Understanding one another's universal needs is the level at which we can connect and find some shared humanity, common ground, compassion, and respect for what matters to one another.

2. Our experience of needs being met or not being met gives rise to feelings. Uncomfortable emotions are felt when our needs are not met, and pleasant emotions are felt when our needs are met. Life changes dramatically for many of us

when we realize that our emotions come from within instead of someone or something else making us feel something.

3. All actions are attempts to meet our universal human needs. What we or others say and do is fundamentally motivated by a desire to express or experience one of the beautiful and nourishing qualities of life that sustain us and our sense of well-being.

4. Human beings inherently enjoy giving to one another and contributing to life. Having a sense of choice seems to be very important in having access to our natural giving. When we have unmet needs it can be difficult to access the natural desire to give. Assuming people want to contribute helps us remain curious about how they might be willing to contribute when we are problem solving together. We more readily stay in the conversation to explore how to meet as many needs as possible.

5. There are sufficient resources to meet human needs. This assumption helps us to come from a mindset of abundance instead of lack. It holds that it is a matter of dialogue and care that determines how we connect and gain access to, distribute, and manage resources. When we live with open-hearted compassion and understanding of one another we can access more resourcefulness and creativity in meeting challenges and needs together.

Key Principles

1. Prioritizing Connection. When I use the word *connection*, I mean understanding what is expressed both intellectually and emotionally. It also includes a sense of warmth, flow, and care. When connection happens, people feel a sense of

satisfaction that you get me, or I get myself. It feels a bit like the plug for the lamp has been connected to the energy source. The light has been turned on and is shining brightly. Now we can see clearly and there is energy and warmth flowing.

2. Holding equal care for everyone's needs. This principle is that everyone's needs matter, and it is important to acknowledge and care for others' needs and our own, not minimizing either.

3. Taking responsibility for our feelings. We do this by knowing feelings stem from our universal needs, instead of attributing responsibility for our feelings to other people's actions or words, or to external circumstances.

4. Taking responsibility for our actions. We take responsibility for our actions by recognizing that we actively choose what we do in order to meet our needs. This means acknowledging that our choices and behaviors are not solely dictated by external circumstances, but are driven by our own decision-making processes and the desire to fulfill our personal needs. By accepting this responsibility, we become aware of our agency in shaping our actions and can strive to make more conscious and deliberate choices that align with our values and the well-being of ourselves and others. We aim to choose based on conscious connection to feelings and needs instead of fear, guilt, shame, ideas of should, or desire for reward.

5. Self-empathy. This is the process of exploring thoughts and judgments and understanding our feelings and needs with warm compassion. We explore our responsibility in the situation, find the beauty of the needs we value and long for. When we do this, we shift out of blame and reactivity,

and we gain clarity, calmness, and self-responsibility. We can then become curious and open hearted toward others' feelings and needs. This is the foundation that prepares us for honest expression and empathetic listening.

6. Self-expression. This is the mode through which we express what matters to us including what is stimulating us, how we feel, what we value deeply, and any requests we may have to meet the stated needs.

7. Empathetic listening. Empathetic hearing and responding is listening to what is at the heart of the matter of another person. Listening and reflecting what we hear they feel, need/value, and would like to see happen while we maintain compassion, respect, non-judgment, and warmth.

8. Protective use of force. This is the principle that when there is danger of physical or emotional harm we move to protect, not to punish. Once safety is attained, we may want to enter dialogue to create understanding and ways to better meet needs in the future. For example, if your child is about to jump off the dock into the lake and doesn't know how to swim yet, you will grab them and set them on safe land. Then talk about the danger and how to stay safe instead of punishing them by spanking or yelling at them. This would be an expression of the protective use of force. Another example is, if my nervous system is being activated by someone swearing and raising their voice to me, I might leave the conversation to protect myself and return later with an agreement to speak without swearing and raised voices. I do this from a sense of self-care versus a desire to punish them by withholding interaction or calling them names or threatening to leave the relationship, for example.

Components

There are four components of NVC that will be explained below. When we use these components, we gain clarity. They help us move into the frame of mind that is in alignment with the NVC assumptions and principles. We use these components as tools to shift from blame, judgment, assumptions, and right/wrong thinking and into curiosity and compassion. We use them to connect first with our inner experience and then with other people.

Observation – What a person has seen or heard that is stimulating a response. Observations are stated as factually as possible, without judgment, interpretation, assumption, labeling, or blaming. It is just the facts.

Feeling – Feelings encompass both physical sensations and emotional experiences that manifest as energy in motion within ourselves or others. They are deeply personal and subjective, representing an inner realm of experience that is unique to each individual. Unlike thoughts or judgments, feelings cannot be debated or invalidated because they originate from a place of raw, immediate internal experience. Sensations and emotions serve as cues or signals, providing valuable information about our internal states and the universal needs that are being met or unmet. See Feelings List in Support Tools.

Need – In NVC, needs are qualities of life we consider common to humanity. These include our physical needs as well as qualities or values we hold that nourish us and help us to thrive as human beings. Examples include love, efficiency, creativity, belonging, safety, nourishment, contribution, honesty, trust, connection and so on. See Needs List in Support Tools. Needs are distinct from the strategies, or things we do, to meet our needs. Needs are what motivate our actions. They are qualities of life that we can understand anyone wanting and we want everyone to experience. When we explore needs together, we often discover that what is important to each of us is beautiful and we may share valuing them. This allows us to respect one another. We can then work together toward creative solutions more peacefully.

Request – A request is a question in which we ask for something specific that will fulfill our stated needs. It is a clear and direct expression of our desires aimed at seeking understanding, support, cooperation, or assistance from others. By making a request, we communicate what we want or need in a respectful and open manner, enabling others to understand how they can contribute to meeting those needs.

Requests differ from demands in that they are presented as invitations or opportunities for collaboration, rather than commands or entitlements. They embody a sense of openness to negotiation and the recognition that the other person has the freedom to choose whether to fulfill the request.

A true request will be free of threat, manipulation, shaming, or pushing in any way. Ideally there is inclusion of the other's feelings and needs as well. When requesting, you will feel open to hearing a yes or no because you prioritize giving and receiving from the heart.

Connection Requests - First, we may make requests that assure us that understanding and connection are happening. For instance, "I'd like to check and see whether my communication came across as I hoped. Would you mind telling me what you heard?" Or, "I am very interested in what comes up for you when you hear this. Would you be willing to share?" Once both people feel heard and understood, you can move to action.

Action Requests - Once the understanding of feelings and needs has been established, you can shift to asking for specific and doable actions. Being specific and clear is very important in making action requests so the person knows exactly what you are asking them to do. For example, if I say, "Can you be more considerate in the future?" you don't have any idea how that looks behaviorally. You may even think you have been considerate. To be positive, specific, and doable, I would instead say, "When you are planning an event for us and purchasing tickets would you be willing to check with me about my schedule beforehand?" Or, "When I have the flu would you be willing to check in with me twice a day with a phone call to see if I need anything?"

Modes of Using the Four Components

Self-Empathy

Listening to your inner experience with respect, compassion and empathy is the foundation from which healthy interaction stems. The following is a brief description of the elements of self-empathy NVC style.

This is an inner process, not one to be shared with the person with whom you feel upset. Use a journal, speak out loud to yourself privately, or talk through the steps with a support person who is not involved in the situation.

Identify a situation in which you feel something, and you would like more clarity and peace.

Let yourself vent your judgments, blame, assumptions, and should thoughts. These may be about yourself or the other person or persons. Listen carefully to what is here. There are important cues to what matters to you hidden within your thoughts and words.

Observation – Describe in a factual way what you saw or heard that has stimulated you.

Feelings – Using the Emotions List, discover your emotions related to the situation.

Needs – Using the Needs List, identify the needs related
to each of the emotions you named.

Sit and be with your needs and allow yourself to feel how you feel
as you notice the longing for these needs and any other emotions that
come up. Now imagine being very kind, understanding, and tender
toward yourself as you just allow your feelings and needs to be here.
Treat yourself like you would a close friend or a child who needs
comfort. You might place your hand gently on your heart, belly, face,
or arms to comfort yourself. You might say things to yourself like, "It
is natural to feel emotions like this. It is okay to feel." "(Insert your
name), is it that you are feeling (insert emotions here) and longing for
(insert your beautiful needs here)? It is so okay to want that." "Your
needs matter and are valid." Just breathe and feel. Allow yourself
space to notice your needs and feelings as you validate your experience
gently. When you feel some relief, something shifts in you toward a bit
of space inside you, some ease or peace, notice that and sit a bit more.

Notice the beauty of the needs that matter to you in this situation.
Notice how they contribute to life, how they matter to you, how they
are unique, how they feel when fulfilled and being expressed. Enjoy
this beauty and fill up with it.

Check for any requests you may have of yourself or others and
anything you may want to do now.

Empathy

Listening to another person with compassion, openness, curiosity,
non-judgment, and respect to understand their experience is how I
would define empathy in alignment with NVC. Here are some of
the key points in NVC based empathy.

- There is no agenda to fix or lead the person in any particular direction.

- As the listener I focus completely on listening and making sure I understand what is important to the speaker, what is stimulating them, their feelings, needs, and possible requests they may have of themself or another.

- There is no "I" in empathy. It is not about my opinions, thoughts, or feelings at this time.

- Simply being present and reflecting the content, feelings and needs the speaker is sharing with me with warmth and care is my intention in empathy. I do this in question form to check my understanding. See template that follows.

- After the speaker has expressed fully and we are both confident that I understand, I ask whether they would like to explore strategies, other perspectives, and requests of themself or another.

- Empathy may also be expressed nonverbally with eye contact, a nod, or gentle touch. Verbal expressions are helpful for checking understanding and we will focus on these responses in this book.

Empathy in the context of dialogue is an important part of creating heartfelt connection and having a mutual exchange about what matters to each person. Reflecting feelings and needs and checking if they are accurate will carry the message of care and create clarity. It is so helpful to make the reflections a question instead of a statement, so the person knows we are checking and not assuming we know or are judging their experience.

Here is a basic template for an empathy reflection:

"When (insert clear observation) happens, are you feeling (insert emotions) because (insert needs) is so important to you?"

Honest Expression

Authentically sharing what is important to you using observation, feeling, need, and request to express after you have done your self-empathy/self-connection is the crux of honest, authentic expression.

Here is a basic template for honest expression:

"When I see/hear_____I feel_____ because_____really matters to me.

Would you be willing to_____?"

I suggest asking for a reflection first round. "Would you mind sharing with me what you understood?"

Then ask for your listener's input. "Would you be willing to share what comes up for you around this?"

After both people have been heard and understood, then ask for a specific action or strategize together.

Support Tools

To support you in your daily practice of NVC, I have included a list of Emotions, Sensations, and Needs. Please use these lists during your practices. This resource can be found in the Appendix on page 242.

Begin Your Journey

Equipment

Journal - whatever form you enjoy for capturing your experiences, notebook, computer, bound journal

Pen/pencil

Colored pencils, markers, crayons, paints to express in your journal or art pad

Art pad or paper

Timer or phone for setting alerts and notifications

Awareness Kickstart

Here is an awareness kick starter for your journaling. Take a few of the statements from each category below and explore in writing:

1. How do you feel when you hear the statement or make the statement? Use the Emotions List in the Support Tools.

2. What beautiful value or universal need are you longing for related to each of the statements you select? Use the Needs List in your resource section.

Have you ever heard someone say one of the following statements to you?

"You never listen to me."

"You only care about yourself."

"You are too sensitive."

"Oh, get over it. It's not that big of a deal."

"You are way too blunt."

"Why don't you ever tell me what you think or feel?"

"You should really speak up more."

"I feel like I am pulling teeth to get anything out of you."

"You are overbearing. Don't you ever stop talking?"

"Why does it always have to be your way?"

"You are so manipulative."

"I am just trying to understand you and it's almost impossible."

"You need to get some communication training."

"I am just not able to trust you. You never understand what I am saying."

Have you found yourself saying any of the following types of remarks?

"I just can't seem to keep a good relationship going."

"I'd like more intimacy, but it just seems like we are always misunderstanding each other."

"My boss told me I need to communicate better."

"My adult kids just don't want to relate to me, and I don't know why."

"I just can't seem to get my needs met."

"I don't know why my friends have been pulling away from me."

"I just don't seem to be able to get along at work."

"People just don't seem to listen to me."

"Every time I try to tell someone something that really matters to me, we get into a fight."

"I get so mad so easily. It is really becoming a problem."

"I just feel so defensive all the time."

"It seems like I have to scream to be heard in my family."

"My kids just won't engage with me."

"I just don't know what to say when people tell me things they are upset about."

"Everyone tells me their problems and I get completely worn out by it."

"I'm sick and tired of the power struggles in my relationship!"

I imagine you could write a whole page of statements that you have either given or received or thought, that indicate to you that something just isn't working in your communication. This guidebook will assist you in taking your NVC learning into daily practice so you will hear or say less and less of the above types of statements.

How to Use This Guide

The daily focus and practices intend for you to start at day one and progress forward in a continuous flow. The attention starts with more basic principles and skills and deepens over the course of the year as you grow in awareness and the integration of the skills. Some topics are a series of three to five days that build from one day to the next. I suggest that you may, therefore, want to start on day one and move through it progressively.

Of course, you may also pick randomly and enjoy the experience of whatever pops up for you that day. If it doesn't seem to make sense to you, look back over the previous couple of days to see if it is a topic in which it would be better to move through in a progression.

There are opportunities for focusing on a particular principle, concept, or awareness during the day as well as specific practices you can do with examples given to build skills. I recommend writing a bit each day about your experiences, insights, ah-ha's, growth, and curiosities. This helps the integration process as you go along. I suggest you get a paper journal to use throughout this year-long journey so you can add artistic expressions if you like.

So, welcome to *Live Compassion, Your Daily Guidebook for Integrating Nonviolent Communication*.

I am delighted to have you join the journey of deepening into self-awareness and communication with others that will enrich life in ways you have only dreamed of before. I find inspiration in your commitment and dedication to living your deepest values through your communication. Having your companionship brings me joy. The more authenticity and congruence we can bring to humanity, the more hope I have for love and compassion to thrive among us. Thank you for being part of this process and working to bring your desire for better relationships into reality.

Initial Inquiry

Take a few minutes now to write your responses to the following questions:

1. What are your current struggles or challenges in relating that seem related to communication? Consider personal, professional, and community arenas of your life.

2. What do you think would change in your life if you could understand your inner experience more fully, express it honestly to others, and listen and reflect empathetically?

3. What would you like your life to look like after a year of practicing NVC every day?

4. What would you like to see in your relationships that honest and compassionate communication could help create?

I predict that your personal growth over this next year will have a positive impact not only in your personal life, but also in your professional life. I am excited for you to find out what that will be for you!

So, here you go! Use your journal to write, to draw, to capture your experiences and explorations in ways that are meaningful for you. I encourage the use of color. Pens, pencils, font colors if on computer. Have fun. Catch your own eye. Let color, art, pictures, words, poetry help you express and integrate your learning.

May you find deepening integration, greater presence, growing compassion, confidence, and more peace and fulfillment in your life as you move through this year of living NVC ever more fully.

Come On

by Kathy Ziola

Shall we go now?
Have we been here long enough?
Or has it been too long,
Sitting, chatting, politely
About nothing in particular?

Shall we go now,
Into the part of us that is deep?
Or has it been too long
Standing, chatting lightly
Unable to find the door to that inner room

Shall we go now?
I'm sure the door is unlocked.
I'd like to sit in there with you,
Gaze and share deeply
About everything in particular.

Shall we go now,
To the center of our vulnerability?
Or has it been too long
Waiting, carefully holding back,
Scared, yet yearning to touch our souls?

Come on! Let's go now.
I could never be there too long
At the bottom of the heart
Sitting, speaking deeply,
Gently opening all the doors.

Let your curiosity awaken compassion.

Daily Practices

1
Curiosity About Facts

Be curious! What is actually happening? Notice and name the facts in situations that arise. Be curious without jumping to conclusions or making assumptions. Name the facts of what you see or hear.

2
Curiosity About Feelings

Be curious! Check in with yourself at least three times today and ask, "What am I feeling?" Use a feelings list to name your emotions. Gently allow yourself to feel your emotions. Any time it is suggested to do something several times in a day, you may want to set a notification or alarm for yourself.

3
Curiosity of Your Needs

Be curious! Check in with yourself at least three times today and ask, "What beautiful needs are present in me now?" Notice needs that are met as well as needs that are unmet. Use a needs list to help you name your needs so you can expand your needs vocabulary.

❧ 4 ❧
Compassionate Heart

Focus on compassion. Stop a few times today and notice your heart. Take a few deep breaths and imagine you are releasing constriction and expanding your heart as you breathe. As your heart expands, imagine a sense of gentle acceptance and care enveloping you. Let yourself relax into compassion.

❧ 5 ❧
Compassion Expanding

Stop a few times today and notice your heart. Take a few deep breaths and imagine you are releasing constriction and expanding your heart as you breathe. As your heart expands, imagine a sense of gentle acceptance and care extending to a person in your life or someone near you at the moment.

❧ 6 ❧
Compassion

Hold in mind today that being human is a challenge and every human being has difficulties. Instead of judging yourself or others for feelings or behaviors, remember that life can be hard, and we all need some gentle understanding and compassion. Remember that everyone is doing their best to meet beautiful human needs with the skills and capacity they have at the moment.

✂ 7 ✂
Curiosity

Be curious today! Hold the thought throughout the day "What would make life more wonderful right now?"

✂ 8 ✂
Curiosity

Be curious today! Hold the thought throughout the day "What is at the heart of the matter in this situation?"

✂ 9 ✂
Observations

Put your attention today on noticing when you hear evaluations or judgments. In your mind, translate into just the facts. What could be seen or heard?

✂ 10 ✂
Observations

Put your attention today on noticing when you hear evaluations or judgments. Be internally curious about what it is that matters to the person who is judging or evaluating. There will be clues in the judgments/evaluations.

❧ 11 ❧
Verbalize Observations

Put your attention today on noticing evaluations and judgments. If you feel ready, verbally clarify what is said by naming the facts of the situation. Name what was seen or heard. Example: Someone says "That person is so rude." You can say, "I heard them call the waitress stupid." Or "They stepped in front of a line of ten people."

❧ 12 ❧
Observations/Needs

Put your attention today on noticing evaluations and judgments. If you feel ready, use the language of needs to verbally guess what it is that matters to the person. Example: Someone says, "She is a big procrastinator." You might guess the needs important to the speaker to be things like efficiency, reliability, consideration, support. You might say: "When you see the work isn't done yet, is it that efficiency and reliability are important to you?" Or "Are you valuing consideration and support in getting things done?"

❧ 13 ❧
Transform Evaluations

Today, avoid making any evaluations. Use only observational language when you want a person to understand the stimulus you are referencing. Name what you saw or heard as accurately as possible. Take responsibility by using the phrasing "When I see_____," or "When I hear_____," instead of "When you_____."

☞ 14 ☜
Feelings vs Thoughts

Put your attention today on the feelings you hear others express. Just name them silently to yourself. If you hear a thought or evaluation being used as an emotion, see if you can translate or guess the actual feeling word. For example, if you hear someone say, "I feel abandoned," in which the word abandoned is an interpretation of someone's behavior of leaving, name a few emotions from the Feelings and Sensations Lists that could be present when the person thinks they are abandoned. These might be emotions like angry, sad, shocked, desperate, scared, disappointed.

Examples of more words used as feelings that are thoughts and interpretations of behaviors include betrayed, abandoned, cheated, ignored, left out, invisible, invalidated, put down, rejected, ripped off, overworked, pressured, stupid, smothered, unimportant, used, worthless, unseen.

You can practice by changing these thought words into emotion words. Here is a template you can use: "When I think I am (insert thought word), I feel (insert emotion word from list)."

☞ 15 ☜
Feelings

Notice when you hear others express feelings today. Make a reflection of what you hear in the form of a question. "Are you feeling _____?"

ᥱᥱ 16 ᥱᥱ

Sensations are Feelings

Sensations in the body are part of what we feel. They are related to emotional experience and can help us connect to emotions as well as help us understand one another's experience. Stop five times today to notice sensations in your body. Just take a few moments to scan your body and see what you sense. You might notice tension, temperature, pain or ache, a flavor in your mouth, some comfort or relaxation, etc. Use the list of sensations to help you put words to your sensations. Simply notice and allow them without judgment.

ᥱᥱ 17 ᥱᥱ

Feelings

Today stop five times for thirty seconds to a minute each time and simply notice emotions that may be present. Just allow them some space to be here.

Your deepest values are reflected in your strongest emotions.

❧ 18 ❧
Feelings Point to Needs

Today when you hear someone express a feeling, given the context they share, become curious about what is important to them at the level of universal needs.

You could reflect or guess "Are you feeling _____ because _____ is important to you?"

❧ 19 ❧
Listen for Needs

Today, listen to the needs others are expressing through their conversations. Listen carefully to others with curiosity about what their need is in the moment.

∽ 20 ∾
Needs Motivate Action

Today, set aside 10-15 minutes to explore several things you did today and the needs that motivated you to do them. Example: I went to work. The needs I was trying to meet were contribution, security, creativity, integrity, reliability, fun, etc.

∽ 21 ∾
Needs Met and Unmet

Today, set aside 10-15 minutes to explore several things you did today and what needs were met and unmet in doing them. For example, today I got up early and went swimming. This met the needs for exercise, health, and fun. Unmet needs were rest, comfort, and ease. I would have liked to sleep a little longer in my cozy bed.

∽ 22 ∾
Needs

Today, choose a need from the list that is a high priority for you now. Spend 5-20 minutes sitting with this need in your mind and heart. Allow yourself to feel what comes up as you sit with this quality of life that you value so highly. You may have a variety of feelings, anything from pleasure to sadness. Be gentle and compassionate with yourself by giving yourself permission to feel whatever you feel. Enjoy and appreciate this quality of life without judgment.

✎ 23 ✎
Needs of Others

Consider a situation in which someone's words or actions stimulated a sense of unease, irritation, or distress in you. Take a few moments to consider what needs they may have been holding as important and were trying to meet when they said or did that. What would it be like to hold some compassion for that person? Be sure to journal your exploration.

✎ 24 ✎
Requests vs Demands

Today, listen for demands. Notice when you or others make demands. Notice how it feels in your body when you hear a demand. Notice your emotional reaction. Notice the impact on willingness to say yes, whether that is to you or you to another. Notice how you feel toward the person making the demand.

✎ 25 ✎
Natural Giving

Today, consider that all human beings have needs and how natural it is. Explore how you have given from your heart to meet someone else's need or needs in the past. How did it feel to do this? What needs of yours did you meet when giving from your heart in this way?

❧ 26 ❧

Needs/Requests

Today, notice a need that you have held within yourself and have not spoken of or asked anyone to meet. Consider how natural it is for you to have needs just like everyone else does. Consider some strategies you might request of someone to help you meet this need?

❧ 27 ❧

Requests for Understanding Me

Today, practice making requests for reflection after you share something that matters to you. "I want to make sure I am expressing myself clearly. Would you mind telling me what you heard?" "This really matters to me, and I want to make sure I am saying what I mean. Would you be willing to tell me what you got from what I said?" "Would you help me out here by telling me what you heard is important to me?"

❧ 28 ❧
Requests for Understanding the Other

Today, after expressing something to someone, make a connection request to understand the other. Examples: "Would you be willing to share what comes up for you when you hear me say this?" "I'd love to hear your thoughts and feelings on this. Would you like to share?" "Would you mind telling me how these lands for you?" "How is it for you to hear this?"

Say What You Mean

by Kathy Ziola

Words of honesty
Come best from the heart
Self-connecting before we start

Discover the feelings
That lead to the needs
Shift out of blame to truly see

What is important enough
To be passionate about
Say what matters and let it out

No blame or judgment
Comes through the voice
When self-empathy first has been the choice.

Then speak with the heart
And the fullness of life
To invite someone in to your inner life
Take courage my friends
As you express yourself
Don't let it all sit there on the back shelf!

When you say what you mean
And speak from the heart
Compassion grows whether together or apart.

So, say what you mean
And mean what you say
When you share what's alive instead of backing away.

❧ 29 ❧

Honest Expression

Put your attention on making expressions today that include observations, feelings, needs, and a request. Examples: "When I arrived after the meeting started this morning, I felt embarrassed and frustrated because reliability and efficiency are so important to me. I wonder, would you like to share about how it was for you so we can clear the air?" "I'm excited about the upcoming party and really looking forward to relaxing and having fun. Would you like to join me Friday night?"

"As I look at the project assignments, I am excited because I appreciate the opportunity to work together. I really enjoy collaboration. How do you feel about it?"

❧ 30 ❧

Honest Expression

Before making an honest expression about something that matters to you, take a few moments to self-connect and to sit with the beauty of the needs you are holding. Notice how unique and beautiful that need or those needs are to you. Notice how they contribute to life. Imagine you are filled with these beautiful qualities. Imagine they permeate your body, mind, emotions, voice. When you express, feel this fullness and the beauty of those needs as you speak instead of focusing on a sense of lack or desperation.

❧ 31 ❧
Empathy and Presence

When you listen to others today, notice what is going on in yourself. Are you present? What is your attention doing? Are you thinking about what to say or do next? Are you trying to fix the other person? Just become aware of your habits today.

❧ 32 ❧
Empathy and Self-Awareness

As you listen to others today, notice how what you hear registers in you. Can you *sense* the speaker's feelings? Can you *sense* or hear the needs that are active for the other? What do you notice in your body as you simply listen?

❧ 33 ❧
Empathy and Availability

When someone asks you to listen to them, do a little self-check-in first. Are you available? How much time do you have? Do you have the capacity to listen and be empathetic in the moment? If not, let the person know your limitations and ask if you can talk at another time, or help them find another resource for the support they need.

❧ 34 ❧
Empathy and Reflecting

Today, listen carefully to others. Practice making empathetic reflective questions based on what someone has said. Check for your understanding. Ask "Are you feeling _____ because _____ is important to you?"

❧ 35 ❧
Empathy

Today, take the opportunity to make empathic reflections in the context of conversation. When someone speaks something that is important to them, imagine they have made a connection request of you and check your understanding. Pose a reflective question like "Are you _____(name a feeling)_____ because _____(name a need)_____ is important to you? Do this before offering your input of any kind.

❧ 36 ❧
Empathy Spaciousness

When someone shares something emotional, focus on just slowing down a bit. Don't rush to get them over the feelings. Reflect their feelings and needs, and when your reflection lands, just be quiet for a bit. Allow them to lead the conversation or let them know there is no rush, and you support them in taking their time.

❧ 37 ❧
Natural Giving

Spend some time today noticing your desire to contribute to others. Pay attention to any inclinations you may have to be helpful, to meet others' needs, to say yes to requests. Just notice whether this is present for you. If it is not, notice what needs of yours are holding the most space in you and wanting your attention. It can be difficult to access our natural desire to give when we have unmet needs pressing upon us. What needs might be present that block your natural giving?

❧ 38 ❧
Honest Expression Withheld

Today consider something you have been holding back from expressing. Consider what is holding you back. What needs are you meeting by not speaking up? What needs would you meet by speaking up? If you were to speak up, what would you say using observation, feelings, needs, and a request?

❧ 39 ❧
Self-Connection

Consider an interaction that left you feeling less than satisfied, a bit unsettled or uncomfortable with the way the conversation went. Take some time to journal a translation into NVC. Describe the situation, then clarify the clear, factual observations, feelings, needs, and possible requests. Consider the possible feelings, needs, and requests the other person in the situation may have had.

✌ 40 ✌

Softening Attachment to Outcomes

Today, put your attention on noticing where you are attached to your idea, your strategy, or your sense of being right. Simply notice if this comes up in you today. You can also notice if you sense or hear it in others. Notice and explore the possible needs behind these attachments. What are you or the other longing for? How does it impact the interaction when someone is holding a strong position without openness to the other and their input and needs? What would it be like to soften it a bit and allow space for other possibilities? Write or express about this in your journal.

✌ 41 ✌

Interdependence & Mattering

We do not live in a vacuum. We are constantly in relationships with others, and humans depend upon and impact one another moment to moment. Put your attention today on interdependence. Notice how what you say and do impacts others and how what they say and do impacts you. Thinking that what we do and say only affects us individually is a misunderstanding. You matter. Others matter. How we interact matters. Notice what matters to you as you interact, impact others, and receive impact from others. How would you act differently if you held the thought that I matter? How would you act differently if you held the thought that other people matter? Journal your discoveries today.

✁ 42 ✁
Self-responsibility for Feelings

Focus on responsibility for feelings today. Remember that you are responsible for your feelings because of the needs that are present for you. Likewise, others are responsible for their own feelings because of the needs present for them. Try owning your feelings by using the following prompts, either internally, verbally or writing in your journal.

"I feel _____ because I value _____."

"I feel _____ because _____ is important to me."

Fill in the blanks with feelings and needs.

Watch out for language like "That makes me feel _____."

"You make me feel _____."

"They made me feel _____." These attribute emotions to things outside of you and we are working with emotions coming from our needs.

✁ 43 ✁
Self-responsibility for Actions

Put your attention on responsibility for your choices today. Remember that needs are at the root of all behaviors and words. For every choice you make today, from brushing your teeth to making that big presentation, take a moment to connect with the needs that are motivating your actions and words.

❧ 44 ❧
Self-responsibility & Choice

Watch out for victim-mentality thoughts and words today. These are thoughts and words that indicate you have forgotten you have choice and responsibility for your actions. Notice inner or outer language that is focused on "I have to," "They made me," "I couldn't help it," "I had no choice in the matter." See if you can find the level where you are choosing to do something because it meets some needs of yours. Identify those needs.

❧ 45 ❧
Self-empathy

Try some small bits of self-empathy today. You can start with simple things like how you feel and the needs you have when it is time to get up in the morning and you have resistance. Just notice your feelings and needs when you feel a little uncomfortable with something. Take a few moments, breathe, name and be with feelings and needs gently.

❧ 46 ❧
Gratitude

Today connect to something someone said or did for which you are grateful. Name the specific actions or words that contributed to you, how you feel, and the needs that were met. Express it to someone if you feel ready. This may also be gratitude toward yourself.

❧ 47 ❧
Emergency Self-empathy

When you find yourself having trouble staying engaged in a conversation because you have become upset, ask for a pause, and take a few moments of self-empathy. Notice any judgments or *should* thoughts, clarify the observations, connect to your needs in the situation, allow the feelings related to the needs to arise and be noted briefly. Take a few moments of self-compassion and gentle understanding of your beautiful needs. Breathe. Return to the conversation ready to listen again or to express authentically. You can give yourself more empathy later if needed. This brief self-empathy is for helping you navigate a difficult moment and being able to move through it with connection.

❧ 48 ❧
Embody Needs

Today, connect to the need that is most important to you. Spend 5-10 minutes in the morning sitting with the beauty of this need, its uniqueness, how it contributes to life, how precious it is to you. Let yourself fill up with the beautiful energy of this need. Imagine it filling you and overflowing. Step into your day bringing the fullness of this need with you into all your actions and interactions. See if you can live embodying this need today.

✑ 49 ✑

Celebration

Today, look for things to celebrate. These may be interactions, accomplishments, learnings, challenges you moved through, beautiful experiences etc. Notice when needs are being met. These may be your needs or others' needs. Acknowledge and speak the feelings and needs present that you are celebrating. Examples: Today I am celebrating getting together with a friend. It has met needs for companionship, support, and intimacy. I am also celebrating my daughter getting safely home from a kayaking trip. It met the needs of hers for safety, learning, fun, and accomplishment. It met the needs of mine for her safety and well-being.

✑ 50 ✑

Empowerment

Today, take a few moments to validate your experience. Affirm that your feelings are valid and your needs matter, just like everyone's. Example: "It is natural to have these feelings when this happens. My needs are important and matter in this situation along with other people's needs. It is okay to feel and have needs. Now, what do I want to say or do to move forward?" Take this knowledge and allow it to strengthen you to take action or to speak an opinion, perspective, experience, or idea that you may not have expressed before. Remember to take responsibility by naming a clear observation, connecting your feeling to your need, and making a request for some connection/understanding before making requests for action.

❧ 51 ❧
Self-responsibility for Your Part

Put some loving attention today on how you might be contributing to any misunderstanding, conflict, or difficult interaction. Put your attention on *your part* in it versus what the other person is saying or doing wrong. Take a good look at how you might be reacting based on your judgments, past painful experiences, assumptions, or beliefs. Take responsibility for your part by naming it and the needs you may have been holding as important without realizing it. Internally acknowledge responsibility for strategies you may have used that were at odds with others' needs. Give yourself empathy for this. You can refer to the Modes of Using the Four Components section in the NVC basics if needed.

❧ 52 ❧
Self-responsibility & Regrets

Connecting with regrets. Put some attention today on when you say or do something that may contribute to discomfort or pain for others. Acknowledge with compassion and gentleness that this is a normal part of being human. Explore the needs you did not meet by your words or actions and the needs you were trying to meet by your words or actions. Sit with your regret relative to the impact on the other. If there is someone you would like to clear the air with, invite them into conversation. Give them the opportunity to share about the impact of your actions or words. Give them plenty of empathy. Share your regret, how they matter to you and how their pain touches you. If they are interested and open, you might share the needs you were trying to meet when you acted. You could share what you wished you had said or done instead.

✺ 53 ✺
Fresh Perspective

Today, practice looking with new eyes. Say to yourself, *I don't know what to expect. I am open to people being new and different from ever before.* Pretend you don't know how someone will respond. Pretend you don't know what someone's intentions are. Pretend you don't know anything about a person's past, their habitual ways of being, etc. Let each experience be as if it were new, or the first time. Focus on what is present in this new moment. Practice being open, receptive, and curious about as much as you can today!

✺ 54 ✺
Authenticity

Put your attention on authenticity today. Check in with yourself before you speak to see if what you are about to share is true for you. Does it include some expression of what matters to you (a universal need)? Practice being real. For example, if someone asks, "How are you?" tell them how you actually are, even briefly. "I'm a bit overwhelmed right now and wanting some order in my day." "I'm feeling well and grateful for lots of energy right now." If someone asks your opinion, give them a true one, such as, "I appreciate your efforts on the window display, and at the same time I would love to see more color variations in it."

❧ 55 ❧
Slowing Down

Take time. Today, put some attention on slowing things down a bit. Don't buy into the cultural demand of urgency! Not much of what comes up is an actual emergency. So, take a breath, self-connect to feelings and needs and thoughts before responding. Tell someone you'd like to think about it a bit. Tell someone you will get back to them on that. Tell someone the topic really matters to you and you want to give it the attention it deserves. Ask for a pause when things get intense. Take time and slow interaction down for the day. See how it feels.

❧ 56 ❧
Reactivity & the Body

Today, notice your nervous system. Notice the physical sensations that come up when you are stimulated or triggered by something someone says or does. Simply name the sensations to yourself, or out loud depending on whom you are with. Examples: heart pounding, hot face, pressure in head, tight shoulders, pain in stomach, sweaty palms, hard to breathe, pressure on chest, narrow vision. Give some compassionate care to just allowing yourself to notice the sensations in your body as experiences come and go during the day. Tell yourself how natural it is for the nervous system to respond to life and indicate stress to you. Let this natural response be okay with you as you increase your awareness of how your nervous system communicates with you.

❧ 57 ❧

Reactivity Behavior Cues

Today, be aware of reactivity again. This time pay attention to the ways you behave when you are triggered, even if it is subtle or just a little bit. You may notice you tend to shut down, disengage, engage more fully, fight, try to prove your point, get defensive, make the other person wrong, raise your voice, run away, etc. Notice your tendencies. Bring some gentle compassion to your experience. Acknowledge how being human can be difficult for everyone. You are not alone. This is a shared experience.

❧ 58 ❧

Reactivity Management

Create a pause. Notice when you are overwhelmed today, maybe even triggered, discombobulated, uncertain what to say next, just going too fast for comfort, or feeling emotionally stimulated by what has been said. Practice creating a pause in the action or interaction. Ask for a moment to compose yourself. Excuse yourself to the bathroom for some self-empathy. Use a short phrase to stop action, like "just give me a moment please." Use the moment for some emergency self-empathy.

✌ 59 ✌

Honest Expression

Today, make at least one full NVC expression in your own unique way that includes the elements of observation, feeling, need, and request. Examples: "Jackie, I'm kinda bummed that you can't make it to the concert tonight. I was really looking forward to some fun time together. How are you feeling about it?" "Joe, when I see you here early this morning, I'm excited and inspired because our collaboration is so important to me. I'm really looking forward to working with you on this project. How do you feel about getting started early?" "Wow, I was so hoping for some support on this and am a bit overwhelmed when I hear you aren't available to help. Would you be willing to help find someone to replace you?"

Speak from the Heart

by Kathy Ziola

If someone or something is bothering you
Why not try – to express what is true?
You're feeling frustrated, annoyed or dejected
'Cuz whatever it is, ain't what you expected
You'd like something different but it's not what's here
There are unmet needs that you'd like to get clear
Inquiring within you may find a surprise
It's all right here. I tell you no lies
Whether it's honesty, love, or inspiration,
You can find it right here, not somewhere out in creation.
Just take a few moments. Rest simply inside
You can feel the essence of the need that's alive.
Because it's alive you can welcome it here
Feel its fullness and grace. It's inside, not just near.
You can bathe in its beauty and feel its caress.
With acceptance and love it's all here, just say, "Yes"!

Then when you speak what you long to say
It comes from fullness, not pushing others away.
You can share what is difficult right from your heart.
With compassion and care you *can* get a start.

Bring understanding and peace to all in your life.
Move together through conflict, struggle, and strife.
Touch that which matters to all humankind.
Speak from your heart and not only the mind.

✤ 60 ✤

Acknowledgment

Today give an acknowledgment to at least one person for a way they have contributed to you. Include the specific action or words that contributed to you, how it has impacted you and the needs met, and the feelings stirred in you by their contribution. Example: "Janet, I am so touched by your offer to help with the neighborhood gathering. I appreciate the support and the sense of companionship in knowing we can do this together. I can rest a bit easier knowing I am not alone on this."

✤ 61 ✤

Interruption Awareness

Today pay attention to interruptions. Notice when you or others engage in interrupting without connection. Notice the impact on the others in the conversation. Does it contribute to, or stifle, or negatively affect the conversation? How do you feel when you are interrupted? How do you feel when you interrupt others and see their reactions? Be curious about the needs the interrupter may be trying to meet. Journal your discoveries with words or creative expression.

✤ 62 ✤

Interruption and Talking Over People

Pay attention today to when people talk over one another. Notice the impact of this way of interacting. How do you feel when someone speaks over you or finishes your sentences for you? How do you feel when you speak over someone else? What needs do you think are alive in the strategy of talking over others?

✺ 63 ✺

Observe Dialogue

Pay attention today to the dynamics of dialogue as you observe yourself and others in conversation. There are elements to dialogue that contribute to real connection. What do you see working and not working? Is there a balance between speakers expressing and listening? Do you or others seem to have a sense of what is important or are people speaking off the cuff? Do you or others seem to be caught by surprise, or fully prepared to engage? How fast are things moving? Can you track the three key elements of dialogue: self-connection, honest expression, and listening and responding with empathy? Are any of these missing in the conversations you observe or participate in?

✺ 64 ✺

Three Modes of Dialogue

When you have a conversation today, begin to practice using the three key modes of communication: self-connection, honest expression, and listening and responding with empathy. Keep asking yourself which mode you think will create the most connection at any given moment. If someone is very emotional, they may need empathy before hearing your expression for example. If you are stimulated or confused, you may need a moment of self-connection/self-empathy before expressing. If you are anxious to share information or be heard for what matters to you to create some understanding, honest expression may be the mode to employ first. Practice, practice, especially in easier conversations, so you can build your skill.

Honest Expression

I had a close friend whom I enjoyed spending time with, sharing deep conversations and supporting each other. However, I noticed a pattern where I was always the one reaching out and initiating plans. It had been months since she had invited me to do something, and I felt frustrated and disappointed. I longed for a more balanced and mutual relationship, where she would also take the initiative and show that she valued our friendship. My heart is warmed by being reached out to and knowing someone desires my company and I was missing that.

I started telling myself stories like "She doesn't really care about me" "She's not putting any effort into this friendship" and "I'm not wanted," which caused resentment and pain. Despite feeling nervous, I decided to have an honest conversation with her. She also knew NVC so while I was nervous to bring this up, I trusted that we could navigate some scary honesty together. I expressed how I had been the one initiating, sharing my disappointment, and longing for more mutuality. I asked her to reflect on what I shared, how it affected her, and what was going on for her in this.

To my relief, she responded with compassion and understanding. She hadn't realized the dynamic that had developed, and she cared about our friendship and committed to reach out to me more. She followed through on her commitment, and I felt a great sense of joy as the pattern shifted. Instead of dwelling in resentment and pain, my heart opened again to the warmth of her care and friendship.

Having that honest conversation allowed us to deepen our understanding and create a more balanced connection. It was a reminder that speaking our truth and embracing vulnerability can lead to healing and growth in our relationships.

∽ 65 ∾
Care for All Needs

Today I encourage you to be attentive to both your own needs and the needs of others. You are learning that having needs is a natural part of life and that meeting them or asking for them to be met is okay. This knowledge is a wonderful new adventure for some of us. Take the time and effort to care for your needs today. In the process of doing this it may be easy to forget about others' needs. Practice considering your needs and simultaneously being curious about and attentive to others' needs today. Show compassion and understanding and empathy recognizing that all of us have challenges and needs. Offer a helping hand or listening ear to help meet others needs while holding care for and meeting your needs.

❧ 66 ❧

Requests & Inclusion

Inclusive requests contribute to more positive collaboration. When you want to ask someone to do something to meet a need of yours today, first have some dialogue that includes finding out what the other person's needs are in the situation. Using your honest expression, share what is important to you. Make connection requests to ensure you are understood. Ask to understand what is important to the other person. Reflect your understanding of them. Highlight all the needs you two have discovered. Then design your request to consider and include both your needs and theirs.

❧ 67 ❧

Needs Meditation

Today choose a need that is one with which you feel little connection and is not much of a priority for you. Think of one that when someone else values it highly, you have a hard time relating to it, and to them. Take 5-10 minutes to sit with this need. Consider how it contributes to life. Notice its value and uniqueness. Notice how your body feels when you focus on this need. It has a particular energy or feel to it that is distinct from other needs. What does it feel like to you? Is it vibrant, stimulating, moving, slow, calm, warming, cooling, feeling strong, smooth, flowing, or? See if you can tap into its beauty and particular energy. Appreciate this need. Notice what life might be like if this quality of life did not exist. Now imagine this quality very present for you, in you, and around you. Let yourself fill up with it and enjoy how it affects you when it is here. Do this a couple of times today with different needs that you are not that familiar with or don't usually prioritize. How might you relate to the need now when someone else is valuing it?

You can use this meditation daily to gain familiarity with the beauty and energy of different needs. This can support you in having understanding and compassion for others' needs and priorities and therefore less resistance and conflict.

≫ 68 ≫

Request vs. Demand Energy

Today be mindful of any time that you make a request. Notice the energy you hold behind your request. Are you truly interested in the other person's willingness and to receive a yes from the heart, or are you most interested in getting what you want from them? Just notice and be present with this tendency if it comes up. Check yourself to see if you would be open to hearing a no and exploring other strategies to meet your needs.

≫ 69 ≫

Responding to Requests

Pay attention today to how you respond to others' requests of you. Do you respond authentically, or do you tend to say no out of rebellion, make excuses, or acquiesce to please others, gain approval, or just make things easier? Be sure to journal about this at the end of your day.

❧ 70 ❧

Requests - Responding from the Heart

When anyone makes a request of you today, take a moment to check in with yourself and see how you truly feel about the request. Are you moved to meet their needs from a heartfelt "yes?" Or do you have other needs present in you that are pressing for you? Once you have checked in, make an authentic response to the requester.

❧ 71 ❧

Responding to Requests

Practice saying no with compassion today when you are not willing or able to meet someone's request. Start by offering an empathic reflection of how important the request is to the person and how they matter to you. Become aware of and share the needs and feelings you have related to the request. Let the person know that you are unable or unwilling to meet the request. Share the needs of yours that you are saying yes to if you like. Offer to brainstorm other strategies that you could do or that they could do. Offer ideas of other resources that could help them meet their needs. Example: "Is it that you are feeling anxious about getting to the airport on time and want support with a ride? I hear how important it is to you to have trust and ease in your travel. You are important to me, and I want that for you. And I am not available to help you out with a ride that day. I have not been well and need rest to take care of my health. Would you like to brainstorm some other strategies to give you the comfort and ease you want in getting there safely and on time?"

❧ 72 ❧

Hearing a No

Pay attention today if you hear a no to a request you make of someone. Notice how you feel. A reaction of anger may indicate attachment to a specific strategy without openness to new strategies or to the other person's ideas and needs. Disappointment may be expected if you had a strong preference. Practice staying compassionately engaged with the person to express your feelings and needs and to hear theirs. This will help build connection in your relationship even when requests are not met. Continue to explore other strategies they may be willing to do, or other resources of which they may be aware to help meet your needs.

❧ 73 ❧

Self-connection

Take a few minutes today to check in with yourself about an important concern, event, decision, or issue. Name the facts of the situation. Explore your needs and feelings related to it. Give yourself time to breathe, be gentle with your feelings and needs, mourn or celebrate what is present in you. Just let your body sensations be here and give yourself some time and space to notice and allow your experience. Sit quietly and notice any wisdom or movement toward action that naturally comes to you. It's not about figuring it out. Just be present and allow the process to unfold and see what comes to you.

❧ 74 ❧
Shared Humanity

Today put your attention on being curious about the needs you have that are shared with others you encounter. Look and listen for shared needs. Notice your needs in each setting and wonder what needs others have in that setting. You may even express the needs that are important to you and check and see whether others are holding the same need. For example, "I'm tired today and really needing some rest. How are you feeling?" "I am excited about this project because I really want to improve efficiency for our customers. What do you find exciting or important in what we are doing here?"

❧ 75 ❧
Power Exploration

Today, notice where in life you feel a sense of power and strength. Notice whether it is at the expense of others, in the service of others, or in collaboration with others. Be as honest with yourself as possible. Spend some time in self-empathy if some of this is difficult to notice. Notice how you behave when you feel empowered from a place of care and awareness of needs.

If you have not had the experience of empowerment having the elements of care and awareness of needs, imagine what it would be like. Imagine feeling strong and confident as you make choices that are based on considering the needs of yourself and others. Imagine acting with clarity and care and respect for all concerned. How might this impact you and anyone involved?

✥ 76 ✥
Powerlessness Exploration

Today, pay attention to experiences in which you feel a decreased sense of power or a sense of being powerless. Notice what thoughts you are thinking and believing. Notice how you might be relinquishing power or self-responsibility. Notice how you behave when you feel powerless. Bring some loving care to yourself as you acknowledge that you have done your best with the conditioning and skills you have.

✥ 77 ✥
Power with Others

Today, focus on speaking and listening authentically. Put your attention on valuing everyone's feelings, needs, thoughts, and opinions as well as yours. Speak what is important to you using NVC. See how you can work together with others to discover strategies that work the best to meet the most needs. Use observations, feelings, needs, and requests to express. Listen with curiosity and reflect other speakers' feelings and needs. Collaborate.

✑ 78 ✑

Speaking Up to Power

Today, notice where in your life you experience someone being in a position of power over you. Notice how this feels to you. Consider how you might behave or contribute if you were to hold the idea that both of you have important needs that inform your decisions and actions. Consider how you might share something important to you with this person with the intention of contributing to meeting more needs while staying open to their needs and responses.

✑ 79 ✑

Power Over Others

Consider a relationship in which you hold a position of power over someone else. This may be at work, as a parent, as a leader of a committee or group. Notice how you feel about this. Consider how the other person may feel in relation to you. How do they respond to your requests or instructions? Do you have the sense they are comfortable with you? Do you think they may say yes with some resentment? Do you think they may hold back speaking up out of fear? Pay attention to your attitudes about being in a position of power and how you interact. How might you use NVC to bring more shared power into this relationship?

❧ 80 ❧
True Yes

Today, notice what it is like to hear or say a "yes" to a request when the yes comes from true clarity, willingness, and a desire to give. How does it feel when you or the other give because you truly want to? How does it impact the relationship? How do you feel about exchanging requests with this person in the future? How does this differ from hearing or saying a yes that comes from fear, guilt, a sense of should or have to, or fear of disapproval or loss or negative consequences? How does that feel? How does it impact the relationship and the openness to requests with this person in the future? Just pay attention.

❧ 81 ❧
Requests

When making a request of someone today, even a simple one, notice whether you have any attachment to them saying yes. Try starting your request with, "I really want to know if you are willing to _____ and would you feel whole-hearted about it." Or "Please let me know if you hear any demand in what I am asking. I really want you to have a sense of choice about it and only say yes if you truly want to say yes."

≈ 82 ≈
Beauty of Needs

Listen for a need that someone else expresses today. Put your attention on the inherent beauty and value of that need in and of itself. Can you find it in your heart to want that person's need to be met just because it is a beautiful quality of life? Regardless of whether you are able or willing to contribute to the need, can you hold care and compassion for that individual and their longing for it?

≈ 83 ≈
Inclusion & Collaboration

Before making a request today, prioritize including someone else's thoughts, feelings and especially needs. Take time for mutual sharing and exploration to build understanding. This creates a foundation for collaboration in which all needs, ideas and strategies are included. Try this out today in any situation where you are looking for action that involves another person or people. Write about your experience.

≈ 84 ≈
Inclusion & Connection

Take care today to include others in the conversation. If you are tempted to make an expression that lasts more than two minutes, consider a pause to check with the other person for understanding. It can be easy to fall into a monologue believing the listener is understanding you as you intend. Remember to check in with your listeners and include them in the conversation. You can use connection requests: "Would you mind reflecting your understanding so far?"

"How is it for you to hear what I am sharing?" "What comes up for you on this topic?" "I'd love to hear your thoughts and feelings on this. Would you like to share before I say more?"

❧ 85 ❧
Inclusion

Be curious about what is present for others. Ask for their thoughts or feelings and what matters to them. When you have expressed something that matters to you, pause, and ask how it is for the listener to hear it. Notice whether you have resistance to inclusion. Explore the needs you might be trying to meet by not including others in the conversation.

❧ 86 ❧
Change Reactivity to Empathy

When someone is upset with you and accusing or blaming you, take a moment to manage your reactivity and nervous system. Take a couple of deep breaths and give yourself some compassion internally by acknowledging your activation, name your sensations and emotions. Acknowledge how difficult it is to receive the blame and negative input and breathe deeply. Assure yourself it is natural to have some feelings about this. Notice your inclination to get defensive and your desire for understanding. Acknowledge your needs for understanding, care, respect, etc. Notice your regret and care for others. Remember your desire for peace and connection. When you have calmed yourself, offer a simple empathy guess of a feeling and need to the person who is upset. Be careful to name their feelings and values/needs versus making it about you.

✌ 87 ✎

Interrupting

Notice when you feel disconnected when someone is speaking. What needs of yours are present? Does frustration build up in you? Are you bored, impatient, overwhelmed, out of time? How might you interrupt while holding care for the speaker and being honest about what is going on for you? Example: "I hear that you have a lot of passion for this, and I am a bit overwhelmed. Would you mind if I reflect what I understand so far before you continue?"

✌ 88 ✎

Reactivity in Another

When someone else becomes stimulated or triggered and their nervous system goes into survival mode you may be able to notice the signs now that you have some awareness of your own reactivity. You may notice increased intensity of voice, rate of speech, shutting down, flushed face, clenched fists, changes in breathing, defensiveness or fighting etc. At this point they are not going to be functioning with clarity and it will be hard to connect effectively. We have all been there. It is time for some compassion. Ask if you can slow the conversation down a bit together. Assure them there is no hurry and you would like to continue calmly. You could offer some simple empathy to de-escalate intensity. Examples: "I notice I'm starting to feel a bit uncomfortable with the intensity and I would like to really connect with you. Would you be open to just slowing things down a bit so we can both catch a breath?" "This conversation really matters to me. I wonder, are you feeling a bit _____ (make your best guess, overwhelmed, stimulated, stressed etc) and needing some _____(clarity, calm, space, understanding for example)? Would you be open to taking a beat so we can both recalibrate for a moment?"

Try this out if it comes up today or rework a past interaction writing out some possible expressions.

✄ 89 ✄
Reactivity

Managing reactivity takes a lot of practice for most of us. When your nervous system gets stimulated, remember to pause in your interaction by saying something simple like, "I'd like to take a moment before I respond" or "Let me get back to you on that in a few minutes," or simply, "Hold on a sec." Practice using a simple sentence to create space to calm yourself. Then take a few deep breaths and simply name your sensations, feelings, and thoughts to yourself. You can also name what you see around you for grounding. Notice you are safe and thank your brain for doing its best to protect you. Then you can use some self-empathy to gain clarity and be present to your inner experience before re-engaging.

Banshee

by Kathy Ziola

Who is that screaming banshee?
I hear the voice coming out of me.

It couldn't be me. I'm about compassion
Yet here I am screaming with passion

Some crazy thing triggered a wild reaction
And without awareness I burst into action

It's so hard to accept my lack of congruence
And watch interaction dissolve into ruins

When so overwhelmed, I lose touch with choice.
Fall into an old pattern, truth gone from my voice

The powerful movement of conditioning has force
I have succumbed time and again with remorse

Now forgiveness and love are required
Condemnation and judgment must be retired
The tears will flow, and the body might shake
To release guilt and pain and to freedom awake

When she comes again, that screaming banshee
I'll remember her voice and that it's not really me

I'm the one listening to her pain and confusion
And when I hear that screaming, I'll give an infusion

Of tenderness and love and plenty of space
Till she knows she is heard and opens to grace

❧ 90 ❧
Gratitude

Spend some time being grateful and acknowledging yourself for the needs you met today.

Name specific actions, how you feel and the needs you met by your actions. Enjoy this richly by acknowledging as many actions, qualities, and experiences you created today to meet needs as you can.

❧ 91 ❧
Congruence & Expression

Today I encourage you to be mindful of whether you are speaking in alignment with your values/universal needs. If you miss the mark, use your journal to explore what needs you were out of alignment with and what needs you were trying to meet by saying what you said.

For example: Imagine I said to a colleague, "Susan is so stupid. I asked her to simply take care of a few arrangements for the meeting. She couldn't even do that right and I had to go back and do it myself." The needs/values I hold in this situation that I was out of alignment with are respect, understanding, empathy, non-judgment, and compassion. The needs I was trying to meet were support and empathy from my friend by venting. I wanted to be seen for my challenges and how hard I work. I feel sad and disappointed that I shared judgments about a colleague with someone else. That did not meet my needs for support, respect, and compassion for Susan.

❧ 92 ❧

Congruence & Action

I invite you today to be aware again whether you are acting in alignment with your values. If you miss the mark, explore what you could do differently to be more congruent with your values next time. If you would like a do-over, write several possible ways you could express differently. Write some possible expressions you might use to ask someone to support you in a do-over. Is there anything you would want to express to someone who may have been impacted by your incongruence?

❧ 93 ❧

Self-judgment

Pay attention to your thinking toward yourself today. Listen for judgments, labels, and evaluations. Translate them into needs as you go along. Notice how it feels to shift out of evaluating yourself and into awareness and appreciation of your beautiful needs.

❧ 94 ❧

Judgment & Clarification

Notice any stories and interpretations you are telling yourself are true about what is going on around you. Don't assume you know for sure, especially if you have a negative interpretation. Take a risk and ask for clarification and understanding without stating your judgments.

❧ 95 ❧

Transform Anger

Consider a time you experienced anger or notice if anger comes up for you today.

Spend some quiet time with your anger. Notice your thoughts that are focused on judging yourself or others, thoughts like what you or others should or shouldn't have done, who is right and wrong, how things should or shouldn't be, and who is to blame. Then notice the beautiful needs which are important to you that underlie the thoughts you identified. Allow yourself to notice and compassionately feel the feelings and sensations that are related to the needs. These are often very different or more vulnerable than the anger related to the thinking. When you feel a shift to peace and calm, open yourself to any requests for action that may naturally arise for you to do, or to ask of others.

❧ 96 ❧

Anger & the Past

Consider something you are, or you have been, angry toward another person about.

Spend some time looking inward to notice what might be stimulating this anger on a deeper level. There may not only be unmet needs in this moment, but also a connection to some pain in your past. Gently bring some tenderness and compassion to the earlier life experience of unmet needs.

❧ 97 ❧
Anger & Self-awareness

Consider something you are now, or have been in the past, angry toward another person about. Spend some time looking inward. Check to see if the other person is reflecting a characteristic or behavior or trait that is within you that you don't like or accept. Bring compassion to this side of yourself. Consider how you might want to be more in alignment with your own values instead of being angry with others.

❧ 98 ❧
Responding to Others' Anger

If someone is angry or irritated with you, remember that they are upset because of a beautiful human need that they are passionate about at the moment. See if you can breathe and stay calm. Do some quick self-empathy if you need to. Take inward time to notice your judgments, clarify your feelings and needs and be tender with yourself. If needed, assure yourself you will process this further later. Then make an empathic reflection of what they are feeling and valuing at the level of their beautiful needs. For example: "Are you so frustrated right now because equal care for everyone is so important to you?" or "Are you pissed off because you really want to be seen for your efforts?"

Coworker Connection

As far as I knew, everything was going smoothly at work. I was having my best school year yet. My students were learning, their parents were happy, and my teammates were talented professionals.

Then, my co-teacher told me she was resigning because she thought I believed she was a terrible teacher, and that I didn't trust her.

I looked at her with complete shock because I thought she was the most skilled teacher I had ever seen at our school! The powerful emotion of shock acted like a switch turning on my NVC skills. First, I connected to my own feelings with a quick, centering breath of self-empathy. Then, I listened more to the distressed person sitting in front of me and I made empathy guesses. "Are you frustrated and want your work to matter? Is your competence as a teacher important to you? Are you feeling disheartened and wanting more understanding and connection as a team?"

I learned that my co-teacher had been getting increasingly upset for months. Gradually, as she was feeling heard, she calmed down, and I started to really understand what was happening for her.

After she finished talking, I asked if she wanted to hear what the school year had been like for me. I told her what was going on for me, and after being heard she was able to listen to me and accept the reassurance I was offering. Together, we were able to reevaluate our communication patterns and identify ways to improve our relationship, starting with the strategy of more regular and transparent check-ins. Because of NVC, we were able to understand each other's perspective without blame and judgment, and then finish off the rest of the school year together full of respect, collaboration, and understanding. ~ *Gwen Tenney, Preschool Teacher*

✎ 99 ✎
Peace

Put your focus today on any moment of peace or stillness that you can notice, even if it is five seconds when there is a moment of no one speaking or asking something of you. Notice that peace exists in the gaps between action and interaction. It lies beneath the thoughts, the feelings, the actions. Underneath it all there is a space of peace that can be noticed. You can see it easily in nature, a blue sky, a bird singing, the grass growing, leaves rustling. These are the simple experiences of life just being life. Within that simplicity there is peace. Notice peace today.

❧ 100 ❧
Peace & Urgency

Life can seem like one big, urgent demand. You may find you easily get caught up believing in urgency, pressure, and demands. It is all in the way you receive and perceive life. If you receive it as an interesting curiosity, an adventure to be consciously navigated, or an endless stream of requests for your attention, you can slow it down a bit and consider how you want to choose to respond. Remember today that most of life is not as urgent as is presented to you. Remember today that you can choose to slow down and receive life's requests and consider them with care, align with values and needs and choose accordingly.

❧ 101 ❧
Presence Using Observation

NVC offers us the opportunity to be more and more present to the moment, to ourselves, to one another. Each NVC component holds a powerful inquiry into life in the moment. Today, pause once each hour for one minute and use one component to bring presence to the moment. Options: What observations can you notice in the moment, what do you see or hear internally or externally. Allow the simplicity of your observation without any judgment to gently settle your mind from stories and interpretations. Just notice, observe, and be. Presence is what is here.

❧ 102 ❧
Presence with Emotions

Continue using the components of NVC to dive deeply into presence. You may want to use your timer for practice today. Stop once each hour and notice any emotions of any flavor that may be present. For one minute just allow your feelings without judgment. Notice any sensations that accompany the emotions. Just allow. Acknowledge the emotions that are present and that they are a natural human experience that comes and goes. Notice that you are not your emotions. They are an energy that moves in and through you. You are the one experiencing them. Simply be present to them without getting caught up in any thoughts about them. Notice the part of you that is noticing and just relax.

❧ 103 ❧
Presence with Needs

Let universal needs be your access to presence today. You may want to set a timer today to alert you. Stop once every hour for two minutes or more and notice the need or needs that are present in you. They may be met or unmet in the moment. Put your attention gently on whatever precious quality of life is important to you. Sit with it a little and allow yourself to feel and experience whatever is present in you. Notice how the need(s) is unique and beautiful in and of itself. Let yourself bathe in the quality and its energy. Allow yourself to notice just being here as you are, natural, aware of precious needs.

∽ 104 ∽
Presence with Others

When you are with someone today, practice just being there with them. Pretend for a few moments that there is no agenda, nothing you need to get or accomplish, nothing to fix, nothing to prove, nothing you must do. See what it might be like to just be present, open, listening, available, responsive without planning, just being. Imagine that your presence alone is enough. You can do this for a few moments without the other person knowing, or you can let them know and invite them to allow you the practice, or even take turns, or just be together with no agenda and see what it is like.

∽ 105 ∽
Openness to Needs

Today, do some inquiry writing in your journal using these prompts. Scan your life to notice any place where you hold a strong position, think you are right about something, are fighting for a particular strategy or outcome, or feel adamant about a preference. Notice how your stance is impacting the way you interact on the issue. Is it creating a standoff, a static, or stuck process? Is it affecting how you feel toward others involved? Are you scared? What needs are you holding with great passion? Can you imagine that others involved are also holding great care and passion for some needs? Could you find some openness to those needs? Would you be willing to slow down and really hear and consider what others are expressing and valuing? What would it be like to be curious and open to discovering the very best strategy to meet as many needs as possible in this?

❧ 106 ❧
Openness to Strategies

Today, take one thing that you are considering doing or requesting someone else do and note the needs that are motivating you. Now before you do it, or make your request, think of at least five other strategies you could employ to meet the identified needs. Notice how this opens resourcefulness and loosens your grip on one particular strategy. This is a path to recognizing and being open to abundance.

❧ 107 ❧
Voice

Pay attention today to the tones you hear and how they impact the quality and meaning of the message being sent and received. The tone of voice in which a message is communicated carries significant weight and can greatly influence our reactions and interpretations. Tones have the power to stimulate or trigger various emotions within us. Being mindful of tones can contribute to bringing messages across with clarity and in alignment with intentions. Pay attention to the tones you hear today and how tone impacts the quality and meaning of the message sent and received.

❧ 108 ❧
Voice

Pay attention again today to listening to other people's use of tone, inflections, emphasis, and volume. Did you feel stimulated by any of what you heard because of the tonal qualities versus just the content? Sometimes it is not what someone says, but how they say it, that makes the impact. What tonal qualities do you find triggering? What sensations or emotions arise for you? What needs are present when this happens? Do you know why it is that way for you? Take a few deep breaths and gently encourage yourself to notice your experience with care and kindness.

❧ 109 ❧
Voice

Pay attention to your own use of tone, inflection, and volume today. Notice how these qualities of your speech create an experience in you and in others. Download a voice recording app onto your phone if you can. Or borrow someone else's. Record yourself conversing or speaking today. Listen to the recording and notice how your tone, inflections, and volume sound to you. Do you come across as you intended, or are you surprised by what you hear?

✌ 110 ✌
Congruence & Noticing

Pay attention to others today. Be attentive to the various ways of expressing including facial expressions, body position, tones of voice, and inflection. These modes of expression convey many nuances of communication. Does there seem to be congruence between their words and these aspects of expression? Does any of what you experience lead you to be uncertain or feel unsettled about the message, intentions, connection, or the clarity you experience in receiving the message? Simply notice when you sense congruence and when you do not. Do not assume you know or are accurate. Just note your experience.

✌ 111 ✌
Congruence & Clarifying

Pay attention to others today. Note your experience of congruence or incongruence between facial expressions, body positioning, tones, inflections, intensity, and words. If you are not confident that what was expressed is what was meant and is congruent, try checking with the person to see if you understand them fully.

For example, "I am a bit uncertain about the excitement you are expressing with your words as I see the furrow in your brow and your arms crossed. Would you be willing to share with me if there is anything else you would like me to understand right now?"

❧ 112 ❧
Deepen Your Congruence

Today focus on congruence for yourself. When you speak, are you being honest and authentic? Are you holding something back and saying one thing and not including what matters most to you? Are you laughing or smiling to cover up your discomfort? Are you saying what you mean and meaning what you say? If so, give yourself some acknowledgement. If not, explore in writing what is holding you back from being fully congruent.

❧ 113 ❧
Empathy

As you are listening today, pay attention to your own body language when you are interacting. Are you holding some constriction? Are you showing openness, relaxation, tension, hesitation, caution, interest, care, presence? How do you express those qualities through your unique body?

❧ 114 ❧
Empathy & Body Language

As you listen today, or as you watch people interacting, notice how their bodies are positioned or moving. Do you see a wide contrast between people's body language? Do you see people in mirror image body positions? Do you notice similar but not exact mirroring? Can you see the difference in quality of connection represented in the physicality between people? How might you use this awareness to connect more fully with people?

❧ 115 ❧

Compassion

Look for expressions of compassion and care today. Notice any small or large expressions of compassion; that lovely warmth of heartfelt care and mattering that is extended by humans to one another, to creatures, to nature. Look carefully for it. It may be in small actions, words, a look or a touch. Let yourself enjoy each experience of compassion for a few moments. Breathe deeply and feel your heart area. Let the warmth of compassion and appreciation for the experience linger. Imagine it expanding like a wave of sweet spring air that refreshes and nourishes your heart, mind, and body. Notice how it feels in your body to be aware of and experience compassion in the world and in yourself.

❧ 116 ❧

Separation

Put your attention today on any experience of separation you might feel. It may just be a small discomfort you can barely sense somewhere in your body. It might be much bigger. What needs of yours are present as you consider this sense of separation? Take some time to sit with these needs and allow yourself to experience any feelings that come up. Avoid going into stories about right and wrong. Sit with the longing for the beautiful needs you hold.

∽ 117 ∽

Separation

Notice today what goes on in your thinking that contributes to any sense of separation. Are there judgments of yourself or of others? What are they? What stories are you telling yourself that contribute to separation? How does your thinking contribute to your behaviors? Do those behaviors also then contribute to, or reinforce a sense of separation? Check to see if there might be a different interpretation or understanding that would lead to connection instead of separation.

∽ 118 ∽

Separation

An inner sense of disconnection can lead to a sense of numbness, depression, or not being okay. Today, spend a few minutes going toward your inner experience. Consciously connect with yourself and what is present inside. Sometimes we depend on the external world and people to give us a sense of connection to life. And life is already present within us. It is not possible to be separate from life because we exist as life. Notice what is alive and moving in you, breath, sensation, emotion, needs, longings, thoughts, energy, expressions. Connection is available. It is a matter of attention. Pay attention to life within you today.

❧ 119 ❧
Connection

Today, put attention on connection to the energy that is motivating you into action or stillness. What would you call that energy today? Needs are expressions of energy. What qualities of life, universal needs, are present in you as a longing, as fullness, as life moving into life? Notice how this awareness creates a sense of being part of life. You: Life expressing life. No separation.

One Being

by Kathy Ziola

I feel it now more than ever
The energy of life that's oh so clever
Expressing itself in so many forms
Still what it is no matter what's worn

There's a flow I notice when I am seeing
A life that is one magnificent being
Same as it is in a tree or flower
Same as it is in the ocean of power

When I hold it all, gently in mind
I feel deep compassion for all living kind
For confusion and anger, hate and sorrow
For separation, pain, and worry for tomorrow

I feel it all as one body of life
With all of its joy and all of its strife
We are part of that one with our function you know
And in the body of life we surely grow

Toward the light of acceptance, love and purity
With trust in the process our only security
I feel it now as my being expands
Remembering wholeness as my soul demands

Look around now at the movement of life
It is everywhere flowing day and night
One part moves and another adjusts
Adaptation, an unavoidable must.

Touch it with me, feel the essence
Of the living organism we call Presence
Every move we make, everything we say

Adds to the experience of the whole today
When aware of this amazing truth
We may choose love instead of being aloof
We may choose to act or sit very still
To consider it all before exerting our will

Feel it now. All that you are seeing
And all that exists is the life of one Being.
Whatever happens and whatever is here
Is a precious part of us, to be loved so dear.

❧ 120 ❧
Connection to Life

Separation is an illusion, a thought, an interpretation of experience. It is a matter of attention. When we are busy looking at distinctions, at boundaries, at lines and edges, we see separation. When we notice that life is everywhere and we are part of life, that every movement impacts life in a ripple, we can see that we are not separate. Notice where you are connected today. Notice how your movements, words, decisions all impact life in some way. See if you can notice a larger scope of life than your usual focus. Practice taking more into your view. Notice one small thing. Then notice what is around it. Then what is around that. Then what is even bigger and more than that. Notice that it is endless. Everything can be considered part of something bigger. Explore how this focus of attention could impact how you interact with others.

❧ 121 ❧
Emphasize Connection

Emphasize connections today. Notice small ways that you can acknowledge or enhance connection. Examples: Gently touch someone you care about. Say yes to someone's expression or idea before adding your own. Reflect back what you hear is important to someone when they speak. Take a few minutes to connect with yourself through meditation.

❧ 122 ❧
Connection to Others

Today, stop at least three times and first notice your own physical sensations, emotions, and needs. Then look around you and see who is around you. Spend a few moments in curiosity about others' sensations, feelings, and needs. Affirm your shared human experience, noticing the connection present in this shared humanity. If there is someone you know in this scene, take a few moments to engage with them, asking how they are and reflect what you hear. (You can set a reminder on your phone to assist you if needed.)

❧ 123 ❧
Self-aceptance

Today, notice the inner critic and judge. Listen to the self-judgments and should thinking that come up. When you notice, take a moment to reflect on what this thought might be showing you about what matters to you. Example: "I'm terrible at following through on my assignments." What matters to me? Reliability, efficiency, competence, contribution, growth. Focus on the values instead of the judgment and see what arises.

❧ 124 ❧
Self-acceptance

Notice if/when you do, or don't do, something today that you wish you would have handled differently. Notice any judgment or criticism or shaming that you might give yourself about it. Take a few moments to give some compassion to yourself for behaving out of alignment with your intentions or values. Acknowledge your humanness! Notice needs you did not meet by your behavior and notice the needs you were trying to meet by your behavior. Be gentle with yourself and reframe to, "I was doing my best to meet my needs in the moment." "What I wish I had done is _____ to live my values of _____." "I am okay as I learn and grow."

❧ 125 ❧
Self-acceptance

Today put your attention on kind and loving thoughts toward yourself. If you try something and it doesn't go as you hoped, give yourself empathy and encouragement, just like you would give to a good friend. You wouldn't chastise your friend. You would offer kindness. Do this for yourself today.

❧ 126 ❧
Self-acceptance

What is the quality of life you most value and want right now? Would you consider this quality a positive or beautiful thing? Consider how you living and embodying this quality would be a contribution to life. Give appreciation to yourself for holding this beautiful quality of life as important.

❧ 127 ❧
Self-acceptance

Today, practice some simple self-empathy any time you become aware of a self-judgment. Very simply note the feeling and need that are present when you hear the judgment. Then name one feeling and need that relates to what is underneath the judgment. Example: "I should have been able to express that without getting angry. Hearing that thought, I feel embarrassed and want to be understood. Underneath that I feel disappointed and long for competence as a communicator."

Notice whether some of your self-judgments sound like things you heard as a child that you have taken on as your own thoughts. Bring compassion to that young, innocent part of yourself.

❧ 128 ❧
Awareness of Flexibility

This theme relates to being in a state of flow and process versus being static and stuck in a position. Today, notice attachments to having things go your way or having people do things your way. Notice how you feel when you hold tightly to a position or outcome and things do not go as you would like. Be compassionate and gentle when this happens. Just notice without putting demands on yourself.

∽ 129 ∽
Flexibility in the Body

Today put your attention on physical flexibility. The body reflects the mind and emotions. Do a few simple stretches while paying attention to flexibility, flow, stiffness, and constriction in your body. Breathe into whatever you notice without judging. This is simple awareness and information. Explore how you can gently increase your flexibility today.

∽ 130 ∽
Flexibility & Flow

Today look for ways in which you are flexible, times when you can go with the flow. Notice any little moment when you adapt to a change in routine or plans or respond to a request by flowing with it. Notice any flexibility that you might experience today. How does it feel to you when you experience flexibility? Be gentle with yourself even if you don't notice any flexibility. This is simply information for you to learn more about yourself.

∽ 131 ∽
Flexibility & Thinking

Put your attention today on noticing any possible rigid thinking. Do you think there is only one way to do something? Do you think there is a particular way people should speak, act, or believe? Do you believe you are right about something that someone else thinks differently about? Do you think your assumptions are true? Pay attention when rigidity arises. Can you imagine there is more than one way to do or think or act that would be okay?

❧ 132 ❧
Flexibility & Creativity

Look for opportunities today to consider multiple options for how to do something. Try coming up with three different ways to do any simple, habitual activity. Examples: Brush your teeth differently, how many ways can you get the dishes clean? Take a different route to work. Think of three different strategies to solve that question or problem at work before deciding what to do. Think of three different ways your kids could accomplish the goals of the evening. Ask for help doing something instead of doing it all yourself.

❧ 133 ❧
Flexibility & Resourcefulness

When someone makes a request of you today, surprise yourself a little and say something like, "Let's think of two more options for how to meet that need, just for fun." You may still do what was requested. You are just practicing flexibility and resourcefulness.

Transformation Through Needs Connection

"I had just lost a dear friend. I had an appointment with a grief counselor and was trying to think about what I wanted to work on. I was feeling lonely and overwhelmed. I asked myself, what do I need to change in my life to feel better? Because of my work with NVC, I knew I shouldn't go to strategies right away. I wanted to spend time with the needs that I truly value and go from there. I made a list of the values and needs that matter most to me. When I finished, I felt so much appreciation for myself. I thought "Now I know who I really am". As I went back and spent more time with each item on the list, really feeling into the vibration of the value, I was flooded with thoughts of moments in my life that matched these vibrations. I felt so much appreciation for my life as it already is, how rich and rewarding in so many ways, and how many strategies I already have in place. I realized I had been spending so much of my time and energy focusing on what I didn't have instead of what I did have. Do I still have things to work on? Yes. But now I'm coming from a deeper place, a more grounded place. I shifted from waking in panic each morning to feeling more certain of my place in the world.

I feel calmer, I have a healthier perspective and more clarity and self-acceptance as I trust and allow my next steps to naturally reveal themselves. I know what I need

will be there for me in the way of support and resources."
*~Connie, NVC student, retired special education and gifted
and talented teacher, ESL volunteer, world traveler.*

❧ 134 ❧
Living Energy of Needs

Each need is so unique, adding its own special energy and beauty to life. Sit for five minutes with a need that you would like to connect with. Put your attention on the need itself, the quality and unique energy that it contributes to life. Notice the sensations and feelings that are present in you as you call this need/quality into your experience. Simply appreciate this precious quality of life.

❧ 135 ❧
Living Energy of Needs

Sit with a different need today than you did yesterday. Sit for five minutes with a need that you would like to connect with. Put your attention on the need itself, the quality and unique energy that it contributes to life. Notice the sensations and feelings that are present in you as you call this need/quality into your experience. Simply appreciate this precious quality of life. Notice how this need felt compared to the need you sat with yesterday. Notice any differences or similarities to the energy and qualitative experience from the previous need. Share about this quality of life with a friend, partner, or colleague to create more closeness if you like.

This exercise can be repeated as part of your daily practice, helping you connect more deeply with all the needs as you work your way through them.

∾ 136 ∾
Needs Met by Others

Meeting needs can happen externally by those around us. Today, notice needs of yours that are met by other people's words and actions, whether they did so at your request or simply by being themselves. Revel in the needs that are met and how nourishing it feels to enjoy these gifts as people meet needs you hold precious and valuable. Be aware of how it impacts you to have someone meet your needs. How do you feel inside? How do you respond to others afterward? How do you feel toward the person who has met your needs? Spend a few minutes thinking about how your life, and life itself, is enriched by these qualities. Express some appreciation to those meeting your beautiful needs if you like.

∾ 137 ∾
Living Energy of Needs

Meeting needs can happen externally by our own volition. Today, pay attention to needs that you meet yourself in external ways, actions you take, things you say, choices you make. Notice the contribution of the needs and how they add to life uniquely from one another. Pay attention to the sensations in your body and the impact on your energy level and emotions. Express your experiences in your journal.

❧ 138 ❧
Energy of Needs Met Internally

Meeting needs can happen internally without external expression! Focus on a need that is important to you today that is not necessarily being met or going to be met by external behaviors or circumstances. (For instance, I may be holding a need for play and not have any opportunity to engage in specific play activities today.) Sit with this need or hold this need internally and welcome its unique quality, energy, and beauty into your awareness. If emotions related to lack arise, bring loving compassion, and allow the feelings and sensations to be held gently. When you feel a bit of space, then focus on the quality itself, just its energy, not whether it is manifest in any particular way. Imagine filling up with this energy and relishing its beauty. Notice how you feel now as you are filled with this quality. You are meeting the need internally now. Enjoy.

❧ 139 ❧
Living Energy of Needs & Speaking

Spend some time connecting to the living energy and beauty of a need as you did yesterday. This time ask someone close to you to listen to you speak about this need. When you speak about it, speak with and from the energy itself. Express how it feels, how it impacts you, what you value and appreciate about it, how it contributes to you and to life. Do this while embodying the energy of the need as much as possible. Let your voice resonate with the energy and quality of this need. For example, if the need is peace, feel peace and speak with a peaceful tone. If the need is love, let your unique experience of love express in your tone and volume and inflection, and so on.

✎ 140 ✎
Living Energy of Needs & Invitation

Consider a particular situation in which you would like to share a need and invite someone to engage in meeting it. Take some time to sit with the beauty and energy of the need until you feel full of it. Then make an honest expression to the person while speaking from that living energy and fullness instead of the energy of lack and demand. Include observation, feeling, need, and request in whatever order feels natural to you. When you speak from this fullness it will come across as an invitation to join you in something you value and love.

✎ 141 ✎
Shared Humanity

Remember that humans want so many of the same things at the deepest level. Pay attention today to what you can find in common with others at the level of universal human needs. Name them in your mind as you move throughout the day. It can be very simple or more involved in different situations. "Here are people going to the grocery store. We have needs for nourishment and health in common." "I see people working. I am working. We have needs for sustainability, contribution, creativity, etc....in common." "We are in this meeting now trying to solve a problem. I guess we have efficiency, productivity, competence, resolution, belonging...in common." This contributes to connection, understanding and compassion.

142

Emotions & Judgment

Do you have a judgment about feelings? Do you think it is okay for you to have and share emotions? Is it okay for other people to have and share emotions? Today, notice how you respond to emotions arising in you or others. Pay attention to any beliefs or judgments you may have regarding feelings.

143

Emotions & Allowing

When you notice an emotion arise today, pleasant or unpleasant, pause, take a deep breath, and see if you would be willing to gently allow this emotion to move in and through you for a few moments. Allow the feeling without judging it or attaching a storyline to it, if possible, even for a few moments. If you feel moved to share your flow of emotion, share your experience with a trusted friend and ask them to simply reflect what you share.

144

Emotions & Curiosity

Energy in motion. Emotions come and go. This is natural and shared in humans. As emotion happens today in yourself or others, become curious about the experience instead of judging or trying to make it stop. Just see what it would be like to be curious about the emotions.

∽ 145 ∽
Emotions & Needs

As you recall, emotions come up because we value a beautiful quality of life, or universal need. Today when emotion arises in you or another, take your curiosity to the next level and inquire in your own mind, what needs could be met or unmet that lead to this emotion? Take a few notes about the possible connections.

∽ 146 ∽
Request & Choice

Sometimes we make demands of ourselves. We tell ourselves we have to or should do something. We may tell ourselves we have no choice in a particular matter. Today, notice if you are making demands of yourself. Write these demands down. How do you feel when you receive these demands?

∽ 147 ∽
Request vs. Demand

Choose one or two demands that you may have noticed yesterday or today. What needs are behind the demands? Could you turn the demands into requests? How might it sound to make requests of yourself?

❧ 148 ❧
Request

Put your attention today on hearing requests. Notice when people ask you to do or give something. Take a moment to self-connect and check for your authentic response. Do you feel drawn to say yes from your heart? Do you find you say yes for another reason, such as obligation, fear, pleasing the other, etc.?

❧ 149 ❧
Hear Demands as Requests

Notice how you receive it when someone asks you to do or give something. Do you hear it as a demand? Try hearing a demand as a request, even when they are demanding. Create a pause or slow things down. Use your NVC ears to hear a request. Remember your own sense of choice. Self-connect and check for your willingness, openness, care, and natural giving. Hear demands as requests. With some demands, you can even respond to the person by translating it into a request: "I hear you saying you want me to_____. I hear it is important to you and I'd like some time to consider your request."

✏ 150 ✏

Request & Attachment

Before making requests today, check yourself for attachment to strategies and outcomes. Could you think of several other strategies to meet your needs? Could you be open to even better ideas that may come from the person whom you are requesting? Explore at least one situation in which you are attached to an outcome. Imagine not getting your way. Do some self-empathy/ mourn your loss. Can you open to a different outcome without resentment now?

✏ 151 ✏

Request - Hearing a "No"

Put some attention on when you hear someone respond with a "no" to a request of yours. If this happens today, use today's interaction. Otherwise call upon a time from the past. Notice if hearing the no was the end of the conversation. How did that feel? How did it impact the relationship moving forward? Use your journal to write about this experience.

✁ 152 ✁

Request - Hearing a "No"

Put some attention on when you hear a "no" to a request of yours. If this happens today, use that. Otherwise call upon a time from the past. Consider what needs the person saying no may have been saying yes to. What needs were they trying to meet by saying no to your request? Can you find some compassion and understanding for their needs? Could you make an empathic reflection capturing their possible feelings and needs? How could you stay in the conversation at this point? How might you express your feelings and needs and stay connected with the other person, even though your strategy is not accepted?

✁ 153 ✁

Answering Requests

When someone makes a request of you today, notice what needs you would meet by saying yes and what needs you might meet by not meeting their request. What are you holding precious for you and for them? Respond based upon needs versus submitting to or rebelling against them.

All of It

by Kathy Ziola

Have I the courage to be just as I am
Letting others think what they may?
"Take it or leave it," I'd like to say
with an honest breath of love

I cannot put only my best foot forward
It takes two feet to walk ahead
And two feet to jump wholeheartedly
Into what is real

The landing is always safe
When the jumping is held with care.

❧ 154 ❧
Scary Honesty

Pay attention today to any sense of withholding your expression. Take some time to inquire, either in the moment or later, as to what needs you are meeting by withholding your input. What fears and needs are keeping you from speaking? Remember the principle that all needs matter, including yours. Your withholding may keep someone from knowing who you really are. It may deprive an individual or group of beneficial input only you can contribute. Try speaking up for the values/needs you hold as important in the situation.

❧ 155 ❧
Group Dynamic

Pay attention to group interaction today. Notice who is speaking up and who is not, including you. How do you feel about the people speaking and not speaking? Is there balance in the group? Is there inclusion? Is there space for everyone to participate? Just notice the dynamics and how you feel relative to what you observe.

❧ 156 ❧
Share the Space

As you notice group interaction today, any group interaction, pay attention to how much you speak up. If you are a person who has strong opinions and lots of ideas and find it easy to speak up, try a new approach. Allow others to speak first. Ask others for their input. Notice how you feel as you slow down a bit and allow others to express themselves. What needs might you meet by doing this?

❧ 157 ❧
Speak Up Effectively

If you are a person who speaks up easily and tends to process out loud, telling your story for several minutes, or working through an issue out loud in a group to gain clarity, try a different strategy. Take a few moments to practice self-connection prior to sharing. Gain as much clarity about feelings and needs as you can prior to speaking into the group and share succinctly. If you want support, ask specifically for reflections or input and ideas. What needs might you meet by doing this? Needs for the group? Your personal needs?

❧ 158 ❧
Mattering

You matter. You may not realize this. There is an interdependence of life with life. You are part of life and what you do and say has an impact on someone, something. Even by simply breathing you are impacting the flow of air, the movement of molecules. When we think we don't matter we may withhold communication, not put our two cents in, not let someone know when we won't be there. *No one will notice,* we tell ourselves. Pay attention today to how you impact life and other people. Look for how you matter today.

✑ 159 ✑
Mattering

Place your attention on someone who matters to you today. Notice how they have contributed to your life. How do you feel when you are with this person? Notice how you appreciate them. Notice how their words and behaviors impact you. Reach out to this person today and let them know how they matter to you and how you appreciate them. You can share some observations of their actions and words, how you feel, and the needs met. Acknowledge and give gratitude to them.

✑ 160 ✑
Gratitude

Take a short pause in your activities today. Set an alarm if it is helpful for remembering. During the pause, take several deep breaths and notice your heart. Put your attention on gratitude for anything you can appreciate and feel grateful for in the moment. Spend a few moments relishing this gratitude. Allow it to fill your heart and energize you.

✌ 161 ✌
Curiosity

Practice asking open ended questions today instead of assuming you already know.

Examples: "How is that experience for you?" "Would you like to share more about that?" "Is there anything more you would like me to understand?" "What are your thoughts and feelings about this?" "What comes up for you on this topic?" "Does anyone else have something to add to this discussion?"

✌ 162 ✌
Prepare for Difficult Conversation

Before having a difficult conversation, it is important to do some preparation. Think of a conversation you want to have. Take time to do some self-empathy to connect with your thoughts, observations, feelings, and needs in the situation with compassion. What are your hopes in having the conversation? Consider possible strategies and requests. Check yourself for openness to the other person's feelings, needs, and different possible strategies. What do you imagine the other person thinks, feels, and values in this situation? Are you open to prioritizing connection with the person vs. getting your way? Draft an initial expression to invite them to the conversation. Example: "I have been thinking about_____, which is important to me. I care about our relationship and would like to discuss this with you. Are you open to talking about it now, or at another time that works for us both?" Adapt to your own manner of speaking.

❧ 163 ❧

Dialogue

Using the situation from yesterday, craft an honest expression to open the conversation you would like to have. Remember that connection requests are your power tool in dialogue. They let the person know what you want back after you express. This can be a relief and a guide in the conversation that keeps you both from going off track or having misunderstandings. Example: "Thanks for being willing to discuss this. My hope is for both of us to be able to express fully and hear and understand each other. When I think about the proposal to spend our vacation time visiting your family, I feel torn because in addition to spending time with them, I also value freedom, flexibility, and new experiences. I am longing for relaxation and also intimacy with you, which I am worried won't happen there. Would you mind sharing what you understand is important to me right now?" Explore in writing or role play with a trusted friend what may come next in your own conversation or use this example to play with.

❧ 164 ❧

Dialogue

Continuing with the situation you have been playing with, engage in dialogue with the real person involved, or role play again if they are not available. First invite them into the conversation, for example, "I'd like to talk about _____. Are you open to discussing it now or at another convenient time for you?" Then share your honest expression and use your connection requests. In this experience, focus on consciously choosing what will create the most connection in each moment, empathy, honest expression, or self-empathy. Stay curious, willing to be moved by what you hear, open to new perspectives and strategies. Thank the person for reflecting and for sharing what matters to them as you go along. Take things slowly. Ask for pauses if you need time to calm down or self-connect. Dialogue is like a partner dance, with many steps as you stay sensitive and connected and flowing together to create understanding. Journal about your experience today.

∾ 165 ∾
Anxiety

Anxiety is related to fear of what may happen. Anxiety comes from orienting to the future. It may relate to past experiences where uncomfortable things happened that we fear will happen again. The part of us that is anxious is doing its best to protect us from another uncomfortable experience. So, it is trying to serve. And, it makes it difficult to relax and enjoy the present. Practicing presence can be of benefit. Stop several times today for a present reality check. Pause, breathe deeply, and notice where you are, notice you are okay in the moment. Notice what is going on. Take a reality check so to speak. If there is something to be dealt with, take the next single action necessary. If not, allow yourself to relish the moment of being okay. Often, we are projecting into the future. When you notice that everything is okay right now, your system can relax. Give gratitude to the vigilant protector in you and tell him/her it is okay to relax in the moment.

❧ 166 ❧
Anxiety

Notice when anxiety arises whether there is a particular line of thinking that you are focused upon or that is running through you. There may be a story you are believing about how something will go or how someone will respond to you. Check into the story and notice how you are believing a thought. Check in with yourself to see if you know the story to be absolutely 100 percent true. Try this phrasing to shift your attachment to the story: "I am just telling myself the story that…." "I am just believing the thought that…." "I am just having the thought…." You can let go of anxiety and fear when you recognize assumptions and stories for what they are, assumptions and stories, thoughts that may not be true. You don't have to believe everything you think!

❧ 167 ❧
Inner Conflict & Listening

Having conflicting feelings and diverse thoughts in a situation can be overwhelming and confusing. Navigating inner conflict invites you into self-empathy and inner dialogue. Become aware of an inner conflict you can explore. Connect with the part of you that says, "I feel this *and* I feel that." This "I" that notices each different experience and set of feelings and needs is the one that will mediate. Let this inner mediator listen and empathize with each part of yourself, just like you might do if you were listening and empathizing with other people. As you do this, be sure to take time to allow feelings and needs with compassion and tenderness. Don't worry about resolving it quickly. Take your time to explore and really listen to the parts of you.

❧ 168 ❧

Inner Conflict

When feeling torn in two directions and trying to make a decision, it helps to come to some stillness first. Sit quietly and allow yourself to become present by noticing breath and body sensations for several minutes. Then hold your situation gently in your heart and mind without demanding of yourself to figure it out right this minute. Consider one option at a time. Notice the needs that are most prominent in the option and sit with those needs allowing them to be fully experienced and held with care. Do this with each option you are considering. Notice the beauty of the needs and appreciate them as they are. Then consider the options again and notice how you feel in your body and how your energy feels when you consider the option. Notice where there is the most sense of aliveness and peace. Allow this to unfold in gentleness and love instead of demanding an answer.

Conflict or No Conflict?

A student shared with me a success in using NVC during a mediation. Two people were on the edge of going to court over reparations for damages following flooding of their adjoined properties. A contractor had been proposed and they were fighting over moving ahead. One person pushing forward and the other saying no. It was assumed to be about the money. When the person mediating made space for curiosity and asked about what really mattered to each person, they discovered that what actually mattered most to each of them was that the contractor do a good job. The person resisting did not know or trust the proposed contractor. The other neighbor actually didn't really know them either. They both needed trust. By discovering they shared the same concerns and values their anger dissolved and they went together to meet the contractor and to decide together whether to engage them. This was a huge shift from being ready to go to court, saving them both the anger, anguish, and further expense of a court battle.

❧ 169 ❧
Conflict

Conflict tends to happen at the level of strategies. People are doing things that impact one another's needs. It can be the case that people in conflict have the same needs. Conflict can be a gift for growth when seen as a positive challenge instead of something to avoid. If you notice conflict, become curious about what the needs are for each person involved. Look for shared needs and acknowledge them. Open your mind and heart to the beautiful needs motivating each person's actions, whether the same or different. With this understanding, invite the exploration of new strategies that can meet the needs of everyone involved.

❧ 170 ❧
Conflict

Consider a present or past conflict. Notice your attachment to the right way to do things. Notice your attachment to being right yourself or to having your way. Navigating conflict requires willingness to be moved, willingness to be curious, willingness to explore new strategies to meet more needs. Explore your stories and assumptions about the best and right way to do things. What feelings and needs do you imagine the other(s) in the situation are/were holding? See if you can come up with at least five different strategies that could also meet the needs.

❧ 171 ❧
Conflict

Consider a conflict you have or have had with someone. Spend a few minutes trying on a new perspective. Imagine trading places with the other person. Putting yourself in their shoes and imagining you are them, use your feelings and needs lists to identify feelings and needs that are important to you as them in the conflict situation. If the other person is available and open minded, you could do this in person, trading places and having your conversation from one another's perspective and experience. Discovering and appreciating each one's needs through this practice can open hearts to compassion and to working together toward new strategies to meet more needs.

❧ 172 ❧
Compassion

Today is an opportunity to touch the heart of compassion. Every moment there is a call for loving care somewhere. Today focus within yourself and notice any positive self-talk. Even if it is something very small. The habitual way we talk to ourselves inside our heads has a huge impact on self-esteem, confidence, ability to speak our truth and show up in relationships. If you hear some positive self-talk, enjoy it deeply and expand upon it. Notice how it feels. Notice how it impacts your body. Notice the needs that are met as you hear this inner acknowledgment or encouragement. Capture this in your journal.

❧ 173 ❧
Compassion

Return to the heart of compassion. You may have some inner self-talk that is filled with hard to hear messages. Notice this today. When you hear one of these messages, use it as information about what matters to you. Use it to discover what needs are important in the moment. For instance, if I hear "I should have known how to do that long ago," I may discover my needs for growth, competence, learning, and/or effectiveness. When you discover the need, you are out of judgment. You can now sit with the need and feel any related feelings and then notice the beauty of the need for which you are longing. Now try on a new thought like "I love that I value competence and that I keep learning and doing my best to meet new challenges every day."

❧ 174 ❧
Compassion Heals

Recall a time when you were going through a hard time, and someone showed you kindness. Focus on the feeling and the energy that you experienced in receiving this kindness and care. Where do you experience this in your body? What sensations are present? What emotions do you experience in the presence of this compassionate kindness? Allow yourself to bathe in this experience, enjoy and take it in deeply. This practice will affect your neurobiology, increasing gray matter in areas of the brain associated with emotional regulation and empathy, increasing your sense of well-being. This allows you to interact more peacefully and compassionately yourself. If possible, express your gratitude through writing to or talking with the person who showed this compassion. Share the positive impact with them.

❧ 175 ❧
Expand Compassion

Recall a time when you showed compassion or kindness to someone or something in life. It may be even a very small act or expression that you made like avoiding stepping on a flower or a bug or smiling at someone who looked lonely. As you think of this act, tap into the quality of care that you were holding and expressing. Notice how it feels in your body, your energy, your emotions, your heart. Take some moments to focus on this compassionate energy and let it expand and fill you up. Remember this sweet energy and the impact it has on you and the ones you give it to. Recall this energy of compassion throughout your day today.

❧ 176 ❧
Impact of Voices

Voice is a powerful tool. The way we use it can enhance connection or create separation. Let's tap into it again as old habits can be hard to shift. As you go through your day today pay attention to voices and how they impact you. Listen for the impact of volume and tone and variability of tonal expression on your body, emotions, energy. Make some notes about what you experience.

❧ 177 ❧
Voice

How have you been doing with using your voice consciously lately? Pay attention today to how you use your voice in different situations and with different people. Notice your tone and how it is influenced by your judgments, opinions, feelings, moods, desires, and attachments. Is there congruence between your intention for connection and the tone of voice and volume you are using. How are your tones and volume supporting or not supporting the needs you are trying to meet when you express today. Now that you have more dialogue skill, you might ask people you are close to or whom you trust to give you feedback about your tone and volume and how it impacts them.

❧ 178 ❧
Experiment with Voice

Today, ask a friend to have a conversation with you and discuss something that matters to you. Record the conversation and listen to the recording paying attention to tone and volume and inflections and variety or lack of variety in your delivery. Notice how you feel hearing what you are saying in the way you are saying it in the recording. Notice whether you are using NVC expressions and responses.

❧ 179 ❧
Use Voice Consciously

Based upon the insight you have gained in the last few days, do your best to use tone, volume and variable inflections to create understanding, congruence, and connection in your conversations today. A few suggestions: If you are saying something serious and important to you, speak clearly, in a moderate tone versus a high pitch. Accentuate important points by letting your voice rise in tone and volume for emphasis. Pause briefly to let a thought land in the minds of your listeners. Increase your inflection and speed when you are passionate about a point. If something is sad or serious, don't smile or laugh. If you want open dialogue, use a tone that sounds curious instead of judgmental or accusatory.

❧ 180 ❧
Rate of Speech

We all have a natural rate of speech that feels most comfortable to us. You may notice variations in your natural rate based upon circumstances, with whom you are speaking, how much time is available etc. There may be deeper conditioning that affects your rate of speech. For example, if you grew up in a home where people spoke loudly and rapidly and there were a lot of people, and you found it hard to get a word in, you may tend to speak quickly to make sure you can participate. If you are uncomfortable with attention, you may also speak quickly to get it over with. You may speak more slowly if you need time for processing or you are used to speaking with people who process more slowly. There are cultural and dialectical differences that affect the rate of speech as well. Pay attention to the rate of speech today and make note of where your comfort levels are relative to rate of speech.

❧ 181 ❧
Rate of Speech

Today, pay attention to the differences in rates of speech of yourself and the people with whom you speak. Notice whether you shift and why. Notice how your energy, enthusiasm level, interest, and mood affect your rate of speech. Notice whether you or others match rates of speech and how that affects connection. Notice how your ability to understand others is affected by their rate of speech.

❧ 182 ❧
Rate of Speech

Today, practice adjusting your rate of speech to match the rate of speech of the other person in conversation. Notice how this impacts the connection you feel. Then play with speeding up or slowing down to see how that impacts your sense of connection in the conversation. This practice may assist you in being aware of and creating more resonance with others, leading to greater understanding.

❧ 183 ❧
Expectations

Have you ever found yourself saying, "NVC doesn't work for me?" This may indicate that you expect an outcome to look a certain way. Pay attention today to your expectations around others' behaviors and the outcomes of your expressions. Just notice what you expect.

❧ 184 ❧

Expectations

Expecting that you will get your way may lead to suffering. Notice if you are suffering today from unmet expectations. Notice whether you expressed your expectations or needs to others in the situation or whether you inwardly hoped or wanted them to be met but did not express outwardly.

❧ 185 ❧

Expectations

Expectations are a bit like assumptions when unexpressed. Confusion and disappointment and anger may easily follow. The key is to make expectations, desires, preferences, and needs explicit. While many people are intuitive, you may not want to bank on mind-reading. Thinking *if the other person loved me, they would just know* also leads to disappointment that can be avoided through direct communication. Let someone know today what your needs, preferences, or expectations are so they can respond to you.

❧ 186 ❧

Expectations

Expectations can be like demands in that you may feel an energy of attachment that stimulates pain when not met. Today, make an effort to express your needs and desires without demand. This involves using questions like this after expressing yourself, "Would you be willing to…?" "How would it be for you to….?" "Would you enjoy…?" "Would you be open to…?" Make clear requests today that include a full NVC expression, so the other person knows exactly what you want and what needs are underlying your request. Example: "Since we've stopped getting together on Friday nights, I have been missing you and feeling a bit lonely. I am longing for some companionship and fun again. Would you be open to exploring a new way for us to enjoy time together?"

∽ 187 ∾
Demand

Check in with yourself today. Notice what you are demanding of yourself to do and any resistance or resentment you hold about doing these things. These feelings arise when we have lost touch with a sense of choice. We lose touch with the needs that motivated our behavior, and we often forget that we chose for a reason based on meeting some important needs. Inquire into the needs behind your self-demand. See if you still hold those needs as priorities. If you are aligned with the needs, remember you are choosing to meet them using a particular action. Notice the sense of flow that comes from remembering your needs and conscious choice.

∽ 188 ∾
Subtle Connection

Sometimes it is difficult to create a connection with someone due to strong protective barriers that prevent them from taking in what you have to say. Fear, insecurity, lack of capacity, judgments, and right/wrong thinking are just a few possibilities. Seeing the deeper part of someone who is in that space can alleviate some of your struggle and discomfort. Focusing on content and the way it is shared can disconnect you. Focus on your shared humanity, your shared experience of life pain and challenges, to help you connect to compassion instead. Today pay attention to two levels of what is present: the content and how that is shared, and the spirit of the person in front of you regardless of how they are expressing. See what you can notice.

∽ 189 ∽
Subtle Connection Awareness

We humans seem to be designed to connect. We sense each other's presence. We can sense when something feels off. We can sense a disconnect with someone even when their words may not indicate it. Pay attention today to what you sense in the presence of others. Do you sense connection and flow? Do you sense that another is having some feelings they have not expressed directly? Do you sense that someone is afraid to share something? Just notice what you sense, don't assume or conclude that you are right about anything, just be aware of subtle aspects of being with someone and take note for yourself.

∽ 190 ∽
Subtle Connection Checking

When you notice something subtle in an interaction or relationship, pay attention. If you sense something, you have the opportunity to check it out from a place of curiosity. Example: "I am feeling a curious sensation in my gut and wondering about our connection right now. I value our relationship and want to check in and see if there is something important that I might be missing here. Is there anything you would like to discuss?" Check out any subtleties you may notice today by checking in with the other person.

⤜ 191 ⤚

Subtle Connection Grounding

Being fully present in yourself creates a foundation of awareness from which to engage. Knowing what is already moving and alive within allows you to notice when something shifts inside you that impacts you due to the other person's process. If you are a sensitive person energetically, the subtleties of this may be confusing. Being well grounded in yourself, you can discern what is yours and what is another's when it comes to feelings and needs. Pause before engaging with each person today and do a presence practice. Notice your breath, sensations, feelings, needs, and energy. Even thirty seconds will support you in grounding before interacting.

⤜ 192 ⤚

Subtle Connection & Intention

Our deeper intentions create an energy that others pick up on. Take time to consider your true intentions and values before entering a conversation today. Any conversation will work for practicing. Take a few moments and focus on your intentions for the conversation, such as mutual understanding, empathy, curiosity, warm-hearted connection, clarity, creativity, connection, and flow. Recall how you want to hold the other person in your mind as you converse, such as with care, compassion, openness, respect, honor, kindness, non-judgment, gentleness, equality, mattering, love.

⋙ 193 ⋘
Subtle Connection & Oneness

The deepest subtlety we can become aware of is oneness. Consider the possibilities of this concept of oneness in relationships today. Here are a few possible perspectives to ponder:

- We are all human and therefore share a certain quality of existence in which we are all part of one experience called life.

- Life is energy. We are alive and we are therefore life energy. Energy is everywhere and is interconnected with all other expressions of energy and life.

- We are intimately connected with one another in a million ways, impacting and influencing and interdependent with each other. Each of us is like one part in a vastly intricate machine. How many types of interconnections can you think of?

- When I act, there is impact, response, adjustment. I am one part of a large system of life that is all moving, responding, adjusting. What I do matters and is not separate from other beings. How am I impacting life today?

How do I choose to speak and act after contemplating oneness?

NVC In a Time of Crisis

I don't think it's an exaggeration to say that I owe my marriage (and possibly my sanity) to NVC. After our house burned down in the Marshal Fire, my wife and I both experienced one of the most difficult periods of our lives. We suddenly found ourselves forced to deal with tasks that are difficult at the best of times (dealing with insurance and government bureaucracy, buying a house, comforting distraught children) all at the same time, while homeless and traumatized. Many marriages don't survive this kind of pressure; but ours did, thanks to NVC. In the moments of inevitable conflict, NVC gave us a way to turn toward each other, instead of turning on each other. When we were tempted to blame each other for our discomfort, NVC gave us the tools to examine our own feelings and needs to identify the real, underlying difficulties. When disagreements flared in the stressful, supercharged atmosphere of our situation, NVC gave us a template for de-escalating and avoiding blame so we could frame the conversation constructively. The patterns of NVC empathy-building language became a comfort in themselves - when my wife said, "are you feeling..." I knew our conversation was going to be okay, because it meant she had decided to step back from the situation and connect. And when I felt overwhelmed and exhausted, without a drop of energy left for anyone, the language of NVC felt like a magic incantation that gave me a way to ask for help. NVC isn't magic, of course - it's a tool for caring communication. But when we were going through hell, it was the tool we needed to dig ourselves out, hand in hand. *~John Richter, Senior Staff Engineer, Google*

❧ 194 ❧
Projection

Human beings tend to project onto others. This can affect our ability to take responsibility for our feelings, needs and actions. Notice that when you are pointing at someone with your forefinger, there are three fingers pointing back at you. Today, pay attention when you think something is wrong. When you find yourself placing blame or attributing negative characteristics to someone else, first look at yourself. Explore what part of your frustration or evaluation is really about an aspect of yourself or your own behavior that you don't acknowledge or accept. Write about this. Give yourself empathy as you accept what is truly yours.

❧ 195 ❧
Self-esteem Exploration

NVC can be used to heal the pain of low self-esteem. Today, write down the thoughts you have about yourself as a person. Allow whatever mixture of positive and negative thoughts and beliefs come to your awareness. Just let your writing flow uncensored. This is simply about making the unconscious conscious. Read through what you have written and notice the judgment and evaluation that is held in the words. Notice where these beliefs originated and acknowledge the pain and pleasure you experience in them. Notice the needs present in your self-evaluations, those that are met and those you long to meet. Be with the beauty of these needs. The gift of negative self-judgment is in the possibility of becoming aware of what matters deeply to you. Journal your explorations.

∾ 196 ∾
Self-esteem

Affirm repeatedly today, "Everyone's needs matter, including mine." Express at least one of your needs to someone in your life today. Ask to be heard and understood, then ask for them to meet your need if you like.

∾ 197 ∾
Self-esteem and Care

Affirm repeatedly today, "My needs matter. And so does everyone else's." Share one of your needs again today. When you share it, ask the other person(s) to share what is important to them in the situation. Brainstorm together how you can meet as many of all the shared needs as possible.

∾ 198 ∾
You Can Shift the Dynamic

It is not necessary for the people you talk with to know NVC for it to have an impact. One person stepping out of the patterns of blame, evaluation, denial, demand, or right/wrong thinking will shift the focus and dynamic of a conversation. Go back to basics today.

When you hear a judgment about a situation, translate it into a clear observation of what facts can be seen or heard. For example: Someone says, "This situation is hopeless." An observation might be, "We have tried ten different ways to resolve this and haven't resolved it yet." Or someone says, "You never contribute to the housework." An observation might be, "I have done the laundry, cooking, and cleaning for the past two weeks while you worked on your hobby in the garage in the evenings."

✌ 199 ✌
Shift the Dynamic to Authenticity

Today when you hear someone say a feeling that is a thought or are tempted to say a feeling that is mixed with a thought yourself, translate the thought into an emotion and reflect or express the emotion using a feeling word instead of a thought word. For example: Someone says, "I feel like you are avoiding me." Translate and respond with something like "Are you feeling uncertain or scared right now and want to understand what is going on when you haven't heard back from me?" When you think, *I feel like a failure*, you can translate and express it as, "I feel hopeless and sad right now because I really want to be good at something." These translations shift the dynamic from judgment to authenticity and deeper understanding.

❧ 200 ❧
Shift to Creativity

Use needs to shift the dynamic today. Pay attention to the tendency to hold strategies as if they are needs and be attached to them. Notice the language of demand that sounds like, "I need you to…." Shifting to sharing needs opens the possibility for more creativity and a variety of strategies that may be appealing or doable for all those involved. Example: Instead of saying "I need you to handle this now," you could shift to, "I'm anxious about getting this done by the deadline. I value efficiency and would love to see us divide the tasks and get started right away. Does anyone have any other thoughts on this?"

❧ 201 ❧
Shift Out of Fix It Mode

Sharing feelings and needs instead of jumping past them to strategies helps create deeper understanding and intimacy and more efficiency. It also helps create buy-in and follow-through with decisions and agreements. Depending upon the relationship you apply this to, you will adjust the level of vulnerability to fit. Practice making expressions today that include observation, feeling, need and a request for understanding. Make sure you have been understood and that you include and understand the other person before talking about strategies.

❧ 202 ❧
Open to Responsibility

Look first at yourself today. When a situation arises that feels uncomfortable or conflictual ask yourself first *How am I contributing to this?* Take responsibility for your part. Have you pre-judged? Did you misunderstand something? Did you act before having all the information? Did you communicate your thoughts, needs and feelings in a clear way? Was something from your past stimulated causing you to react instead of responding? Did you forget something important? Share your responsibility with the other to create some understanding before focusing on how they contributed to the situation.

❧ 203 ❧
Shift the Dynamic

Practice making requests today. Ask if the person is willing, open to, would enjoy, would feel comfortable with, could live with _____ to meet your stated needs. Remember that you want the person to respond honestly from the heart and that you are open to receiving yes or no. This practice will shift the dynamic of resentment, oppression, anger, and disconnection. Journal about your experience.

∽ 204 ∾
Request

Using requests is a power tool in dialogue. It helps you build a foundation of understanding. Remember connection requests today! When you express something and are hoping for a response, let the person know what you would like back. Do you want to check and make sure you have been understood? Do you want to know and understand what comes up for the listener when you say that? Make a request for a reflection of understanding or for them to express what is up for them. This shifts the dynamic of reactivity based upon assumptions and misunderstandings. For example: "I'd like to make sure I have expressed clearly, would you be willing to share what you got from what I just said?" This request may guide a person to reflect for you. You can see what they understood and whether it matches what you intended. This will avoid reactions based on a misunderstanding. If you just plop your expression out there without a request, your listener may do a lot of things you don't enjoy, like give advice, defend themselves, minimize your experience, or tell you a story.

∽ 205 ∾
Naturalizing Your NVC

Sometimes we feel a bit mechanical or sound odd to others when we are learning NVC. Today, practice making some NVC expressions using observation, feeling, need and request by changing up the order in which you use them. A few examples: "I'm so stressed and overwhelmed right now when I think about all I have to do this week. I really need some support. Would you be open to brainstorming how we can share the load a bit here?" "Would you mind just listening to me for a few minutes and reflecting back on what you hear afterward? I'm feeling confused about a decision and could really use some empathy." Mix it up and play with different ways of including the components. You may sense a more natural flow.

❧ 206 ❧
Naturalizing Your NVC

Another way to bring a more natural flow to your NVC expression is to fill in more than just feelings and needs when you are empathizing. Try paraphrasing content along with feelings and needs reflections. Example: Instead of, "Are you flustered because respect is important to you?" try "Are you flustered when you unexpectedly meet someone you respect for the first time? Are first impressions important to you for being seen for who you really are and you wished you could have had some warning that Sam was going to be at the event?"

❧ 207 ❧
Naturalizing Your NVC

Naturalize your expression of how you feel by simply saying the feeling itself without saying the word *feeling*. This can create more ease for you listeners, especially if they aren't as comfortable with feelings. Example: "I'm frustrated," "Whew, I'm tired!" "I'm so excited!" Allow your personality to come through in your voice and body language.

❧ 208 ❧

Naturalizing Your NVC

The word *need* can bring up many negative connotations and thus be difficult for people to receive. Today, try expressing needs without using the word *need*. Example phrases that you can fill in with the need itself:

I thrive on_____.

I long for_____.

I value_____.

_____is important to me.

I love_____.

_____is a priority of mine.

❧ 209 ❧

Naturalizing Your NVC

Expressing needs by defining them instead of using just one word can also help you bring your personality into your NVC expressions. Try expanding your expression of needs today in that way. Example: Instead of saying "…because reliability is important to me," you would say "…..because I want to be consistent in a way that people can trust." Practice using your own way of saying things while maintaining an inner awareness of the need that matters to you.

❧ 210 ❧

Naturalizing Your NVC

NVC can sound mechanical when we are most concerned about getting it right or doing it right. Sometimes it can feel like the NVC police are in your head controlling everything you say to such an extent that you don't speak much at all. Relax today. Focus your attention on your heart and connect with the passion you have for what matters to you. Hold the NVC components in mind and express them from your heart. See how this feels today and note your experiences.

❧ 211 ❧

Naturalizing Your NVC

Return to remembering the beauty of the needs you would like to express today. Each need has its unique energy and contribution to life. Before expressing a need today, take a few moments to tune into that uniqueness and beautiful energy. When you speak, allow that energy to fill your body and your voice again. This will bring aliveness to your honest expression or empathic reflection instead of a rote expression of the right word.

❧ 212 ❧

Naturalizing Your NVC

Being aware of, and adapting to, the setting and culture in which you are speaking can support your ease of connection. In a setting where people rarely talk about feelings or share more personally, it may create disconnection if you use the words feelings or needs. You can adapt the level of intimacy in your expression and reflections by authentically selecting words that fit the norms of the situation and relationships. For example, instead of reflecting "Are you feeling terrified and vulnerable every time you show up for work because you have a need for security?" you might say, "Are you nervous because security is important and there have been some layoffs lately?" Pay attention to settings and norms today and try adapting your language to fit while still being authentic.

❧ 213 ❧

Naturalizing Your NVC

Practice today: Before expressing something important to someone, take a few moments and drop into your heart. Hold in your heart how the person matters to you as a human being, dip into your reservoir of compassion and care, connect with your needs and feelings in the sense of what you love and want to share in the relationship. Remember intentions for curiosity and connection. Then speak from your heart and allow it to flow naturally. Let those qualities guide and imbue your expression.

∽ 214 ∾
It's Not Always Personal

Gaining access to the natural giving that lives in other people can be a challenge at times. Sometimes when we make a request, the person is in pain with many unmet needs and the capacity and willingness to give is unavailable. We can be tempted to take this personally. It is more often about the other's unmet needs. If you are frequently hearing "no" from a person in your life, they may be focusing on an abundance of unmet needs of their own. These unmet needs may or may not be related to you and your relationship with them. If you hear "no" to a request today, check with the person about what other needs are important to them at the moment. Be ready with some empathy for them and their needs.

∽ 215 ∾
Natural Giving

It can be hard to access our own natural desire to give when our unmet needs are piling up. Staying current with self-empathy and awareness of our needs can support us in being more available to give. Notice any tendency to feel resistant when someone asks you to give your time, attention, energy, or actions. Give yourself some empathy for the needs that you long to have met in the situation. Allow and be compassionate with yourself today. You may choose to express your needs instead of simply resisting or saying no from a feeling of grumpiness or irritation.

❧ 216 ❧
Natural Giving

Losing sight of natural giving happens to so many of us. It is easy to hear a demand, even when a true request is being made. Do you react to a perceived demand with submission or rebellion? Neither reaction comes from a heart-centered choice. Practice hearing requests instead of demands, even when presented as demands. Remember you have the choice, and you can choose from your heart instead of submitting or rebelling. You can practice checking in with the other person around whether they are open to a yes or a no.

❧ 217 ❧
Rebellion

Rebellion comes alive when a person hears demand and does not feel a sense of choice. Chances are good that if you are asking and someone is rebelling/pushing back, you may have communicated in a way that was a demand or there was demand energy in your request. You may have forgotten to include your beautiful needs or forgotten to ask for willingness or input from them. Check for this omission on your part. Check with the person to see if they heard a demand. Let them know you want them to answer truly and to respond from the heart based on the needs they hear.

∞ 218 ∞

Submission

Submission often comes into play when there is a power differential, real or perceived. You may find yourself submitting to a request when you have needs, or even strategies you think may be better, but you have some fear. You may fear rejection of you or your ideas, not wanting to upset someone in a position of power or make waves for fear of embarrassment or retribution. Pay attention to whether you feel submission today. Self-empathize. Offer an authentic response to the request and say what is up for you instead of submitting without sharing.

∞ 219 ∞

Submission

If you are in the position of power in a relationship and you sense someone is being submissive, you can express yourself honestly. Try letting the person know that it is important to you to hear and understand what is also important to them. Assure them that you want them on board with any strategies chosen so they feel good, comfortable, or even enthusiastic, about the choices. Let them know if you want to hear any objections, concerns, or ideas so they are included in decision making that involves them.

❧ 220 ❧
Submission

When someone yields their own desires, needs, or opinions, without asserting themselves or advocating for their interests there are consequences to the relationship, group, family, or organization. While submission may be efficient at the moment, it is likely to seed resentment. Each time submission takes place, that seed is nourished and grows. Resentment has long-term implications for harmony and collaboration. Relationships can become strained, trust deteriorates, innovation, problem solving, and open communication are hindered. When someone submits, we also miss out on that person's important resources and contributions. Be mindful today of any submission energy that you or another may demonstrate. Be honest about your desire for true understanding and cooperation that comes from the heart, not from the mindset of "should."

❧ 221 ❧
Forgiveness

When someone's words or actions stimulate pain in us, we may hold onto that pain and suffer over time. NVC can help us remember the inherent innocence of people trying to meet their beautiful human needs. When someone meets their needs without consideration or understanding for us, impact can linger until the pain is met with empathy. If you have someone you would like to forgive today, allow yourself to compassionately feel your pain as you connect to the needs you hold precious in the situation. Allow this empathic attention to yourself for today. The trick is to step out of rerunning the story of what happened and all the "should thoughts" and lovingly be with the sensations and emotions in your body.

∞ 222 ∞

Forgiveness

Consider where you would like to bring forgiveness into your experience. If you would like help in letting go of the pain of unmet needs, talking to the person who stimulated the pain is a potential option, depending upon their availability. You could let the person know you have some pain you would like to express and have reflected, asking if they feel open to listening and having a healing conversation. Do your best to express observation, feelings, needs versus blaming the person. "When I think about the experience of _____, I feel _____ because I so long for _____." Share your pain with responsibility. Invite them to reflect on what they have heard, how they feel hearing it. Share more if needed and ask for reflection. Ask to understand them more fully if you are ready. You remembering each person's innate innocence in this process is very helpful. We all do things that cause pain and are out of alignment with our values. Letting go of our anger and hurt heals our own hearts and brings freedom back. We can do so through inner work as well as relational healing conversation.

Reconciliation

I was on an organization's board of directors in which the board members all lived in a local area, and I lived four and a half hours away. One member was trying to plan an in-person meeting and asked for an email response to her suggested timing. I didn't respond thinking my input wouldn't make a difference being so far away that I probably wouldn't attend anyway. A couple of days later I received an email that was sent to the group in which she expressed feeling hurt at not receiving responses. She wanted consideration, respect, and reliability from us group members. She wanted to know that she and her efforts were valued.

I remember feeling embarrassed and somewhat guilty for not having responded. I took some time for self-empathy to connect with my feelings and what mattered to me. I discovered that I valued consideration and respect for her as well as being responsive in our relationship. I also realized that I thought I didn't matter and that my participation wasn't important. I had not thought of the impact of that on her at all. I didn't think there would be one. I did not write her back... without hesitation, I picked up the phone to talk with her voice to voice. I asked her to share more about how she felt. I listened with compassion and reflected with empathy. I expressed my care for her and our relationship. Then I shared my deep regret for the impact on her that my not responding had had and what I wished I had done instead. When she had received all of that, I then shared with her vulnerably what I had learned about myself and my thinking that I did not matter. I shared how I learned about impact and that I, and we, matter to one another more than we know. She listened and offered empathic reflections to me.

Being in integrity with my values for consideration and responsiveness is important to me and knowing I matter is foundational to being able to live congruently. It was not easy to pick up that phone, but she was grateful for our healing conversation. So was I. Our mutual care and understanding deepened and our friendship grew.

❧ 223 ❧
Self-forgiveness

Self-forgiveness can be a tough one. Notice something you have done that you regret. Spend some time doing self-empathy. Bring compassion to your humanness. You are always speaking and acting to meet beautiful universal human needs. Sometimes the skillfulness is not yet developed, or your capacity is low. It happens to all of us. Could you be gentle with yourself today and give some understanding to yourself? Treat yourself as you would treat a friend who had fallen short, being very kind and empathic toward them. Ask yourself whether you would be willing to understand and remember your innocence.

❧ 224 ❧
Invite Forgiveness

Take your self-forgiveness to the next level today. After giving yourself empathy for what you have said or done that may have been painful to another, invite a conversation to clear the air. Ask the other to share how they have been impacted. Give them plenty of empathy until they feel fully understood. Express your regret and your care for them and acknowledge the impact your words or actions have had. Share how you were out of alignment with the values you hold. If they are open and interested, share the needs you were attempting to meet and what you wish you had done differently.

❧ 225 ❧
Celebrate with Others

When we share in someone else's celebration it is a gift to them and to yourself as it brings the warmth of sharing joy. When someone shares something they are happy about like an accomplishment, a success, or a delightful experience, practice responding with empathic reflection of the feelings and needs they are enjoying. Be the companion in their celebration today.

∾ 226 ∾
Invite Celebration

Sharing in life's successes and joys can be deepened using NVC. Try using all the components to share about something you are excited about, have had success in, or enjoyed fully. Make a request for connection to let the person know you would like the companionship that empathic reflection provides even for the positive life experiences. Example: "I am so thrilled that I have been accepted to the internship up in Alaska. I am going to learn so much working with professionals I admire. And I will be with other interns from around the world on this adventure. I am so excited! Would you mind reflecting for me for a moment? I'd love to know what you are hearing."

∾ 227 ∾
When Yes Means No

When you make a request of someone and they say yes, you can often tell if it is not from the heart. You may notice they lower their eyes or head when they say "yes." They may say "yes" softly or say "okay" with a tone you recognize as meaning "Well, okay, if I have to." They may say something like, "Yes, you know I have a lot to do, but I guess I owe you one." It may be coming from fear of rejection or negative consequences, a need for approval, a desire to please, or some other constriction. There is a cost to a yes that is not from the heart! The result can be resentment, awkwardness, or disconnection in the long run. It may be hard to discern. Try checking in with a person who says yes yet you detect some hesitation or energy of submission or a hint of fear or resentment. Try saying something like, "I want to check and make sure whether you are hearing any demand from me. I really want you to have a sense of choice because our relationship matters to me. How is it for you to consider saying yes to this?"

✆ 228 ✆
When No Means Yes

Hearing a "no" to a request can stimulate pain, disappointment, frustration, sadness, and anger. We've all been there. We just want something a certain way, but the answer is "no." Ouch! When someone says no to a strategy you request, you have an opportunity to get curious! Find out what needs they are saying yes to when they say no to your request. There is always a beautiful need that is present for the person. That is what they are prioritizing and saying yes to that leads them to say no to your request. You do not have to take it personally. You are not necessarily being rejected. It is most likely they have another need pressing that requires their attention. It is not necessarily that they don't care or don't want to give to you. Their giving is simply not available due to other needs taking precedence that they are saying yes to.

When you hear someone say "no" to a request today, get curious about their important needs. If it is your request, ask them what is important to them and explore together. You can then explore other strategies they might be open to saying yes to. If you are observing someone else's interaction, become curious in your own mind. Check in with them only if your participation in the conversation is welcome and appropriate.

✎ 229 ✎

Wallow or Transform?

There is a difference between wallowing in feelings and being truly present with them. Today notice how your feelings relate to the thoughts, assumptions, stories, and judgments that you hold tightly as real. These thoughts are likely to lead to a range of feelings in the arena of anger. Pay attention to the impact of your thoughts on the emotions you are experiencing. Did you find a connection? Write about what you experience.

Your deepest values are reflected in your strongest emotions.

❧ 230 ❧

Wallow or Transform?

Wallowing, or getting stuck in emotions, happens when we focus on feelings that are related to judgments and assumptions. Continuing to think and believe the thoughts leads to a cycle of affirming the stories and perpetuating the related emotions. Use the thoughts as hints to the values/needs you are passionate about as the key to transformation. When you discover the needs within the judgments and stories, sit with them compassionately and notice a different flavor of emotions arising. Bring kindness and empathy to this experience and allow the energy to move as it will. Notice and write about what happens for you.

❧ 231 ❧

Wallow or Transform?

It is the quality of loving presence we bring to our experience that allows transformation. Non-judgment, willingness to experience your deeper emotions, and being tender and understanding with your very vulnerable humanness can support you deeply. When a feeling is hanging around and you can't move through it, notice whether you are judging the feeling and trying to shake it! Allowing the feeling to be here, along with the sensations, is the way through. When you give yourself gentle compassion, the energy can move instead of hide, constrict, or shut down. Awareness of your needs and longing for beautiful qualities will naturally arise. Wisdom bubbles up from this space of peace and acceptance. Resourcefulness is readily available here. Today, simply allow emotions without attaching them to thoughts. Don't identify with the thoughts. Allow emotion and awareness of beautiful needs. Journal about your experience.

✎ 232 ✎
Wallow or Transform?

The simplicity of being is deeply nourishing. Even holding an attachment, desire, or expectation for transformation can create constriction. Your willingness to be present with whatever is here, without any self-demand to be different, can bring about a natural process of life moving as life. Whatever is present may shift or transform in its own time, or not. Being compassionate with whatever takes place is most important. This way, whatever you experience is done so with presence, care, kindness instead of judgment and suffering. Notice any judgment you have today of yourself or an experience that you think you "should transform" or "make better." What would it be like to move toward the experience with love instead of making it wrong and having to change it or yourself? Could you just be with it? Whatever comes today, just be with it. Notice the feelings, the sensations, the beautiful needs, and values you long for. Embrace what is here with open arms and a welcoming and gentle heart. Write about what this is like for you.

❧ 233 ❧
Making Agreements Conscious

Today, I invite you to explore making agreements with awareness and care. Pay attention to any agreement you make today, even if it is something very small that you promise to do. See if you can identify the needs you are saying yes to when you make this agreement. Is it care, consideration, support, peace, efficiency, harmony, reliability, or…? The idea is to be as conscious as possible about making agreements, basing them on connection to needs, whether yours or the other person's.

❧ 234 ❧
Making Agreements from the Heart

When you make an agreement, it is a form of saying yes. If you do so from the heart and from connection to needs, you are more likely to find pleasure in following through with your agreement than if you agree to something without including your needs. There may be conscious or unconscious resistance to keeping the agreement if your needs are not included. You may do things late or not at all, feel stress about it, and stimulate upset feelings in others with whom you have the agreement. Take time to check in on your current agreements and see if you are fully aligned with having made them with inclusion of your needs. Write about this in your NVC journal for clarity. Do you find pleasure or satisfaction in your agreements today? Do you find yourself resisting or procrastinating? Do you find yourself thinking you shouldn't have to do it? Have your current agreements been made from your heart? Pay attention to what is present and make note of your experience.

❧ 235 ❧

Making Agreements Inclusive

When creating an agreement with others, it is important to make sure all the needs are on the table. If you make an agreement with a group or individual without first hearing their needs, it may not feel like a full-hearted agreement to the other(s). In coming to any agreement today, explicitly invite input from everyone involved. Write it down. Include as many needs as possible in the agreement that is formed. Notice how this impacts the follow-through and open heartedness of all involved. For instance, partners planning the weekend may each have individual needs as well as needs related to the partnership. One partner may need peace, relaxation, rejuvenation, and connection. The other may need fun, order and efficiency and intimacy. They may come up with an agreement that includes sleeping in late, going out for breakfast, and going to the beach on Saturday and on Sunday organizing the garage and the spare room followed by watching a movie and ordering pizza. This agreement includes the needs of both instead of one person demanding they focus only on their needs.

❧ 236 ❧

Breaking/Changing Agreements

Sometimes we have agreed to something and our needs or connection to the needs change with time and the agreement no longer fits for us. Abandoning the agreement can seem like the easy way out. It is tempting to just not do it anymore and not say anything about it. This can create conflict with the people you have made the agreement with. If you feel out of alignment with an agreement you have made, take some time to really delve into what has changed. What needs are present now? What has changed for you? What new needs are you wanting to meet instead now? Explore fully. As you journal today, notice and be with any emotions and sensations that arise as you write. Identify the needs that are not met by the agreement at this time. Honestly explore the needs you were meeting at the time you chose to make the agreement. Write some possible expressions about the shift you have discovered regarding your agreement.

✎ 237 ✎
Breaking/Changing Agreements

Imagine breaking or changing an agreement using the expression you created yesterday. Consider the impact of this change on the others involved. What feelings and needs may be present for them? What empathic reflections might you make in dialogue with them? Write through or try out this conversation including empathic reflections.

✎ 238 ✎
Breaking/Changing Agreements

Once aware that you want to break an agreement due to changes in needs, capacity, willingness etc., it is time to communicate. Breaking agreements unconsciously can cause conflict and separation. If you would like to change an agreement about something, create an honest expression using observation, feelings, needs, and requests to connect with those involved. Practice, write through, or role play an honest expression or dialogue using a current, past, or future situation. Now you can bring your awareness to the person(s) with whom you have the agreement. Honestly express using your NVC.

Share the needs and feelings you have about this. Share empathy for the impact of your words and actions on the other(s). Express any regrets you may have about changing the agreement. Propose a new strategy that you are comfortable with and see if it is acceptable for meeting the others' needs.

❧ 239 ❧
Intention

When you think about interacting with someone in particular today, what is your intention for the interaction? Explore this now. What qualities would you like to bring to the conversation?

What qualities would you like the other(s) to bring forward in the conversation? How can you support the process so these qualities can show up? How might you share and invite this intentionality? Write about this.

❧ 240 ❧
Intention

Focus on your intention for connection and understanding today. Forget about strategies for a while and simply express and listen purely for understanding. Only consider and explore strategies after you've attained full understanding.

❧ 241 ❧
Intention for Compassion

Today, focus on the intention of holding compassion as you interact. Focus on the thought that all anyone is saying or doing is an attempt to meet a beautiful need, just like you. Recognizing this shared experience and our innocence as people trying to meet beautiful needs engenders compassion. Allow your heart to open in compassion today. Set an alarm or phone notification for once an hour. Take a few moments each hour and pause, take some deep breaths, and say the word compassion inwardly or out loud depending upon your location. Imagine you are breathing the energy of compassion into your heart and as you exhale you are sharing it with anyone in particular you choose or to a group, situation, or the world in general.

❧ 242 ❧
Intention to Connect

Hold the intention today to make connection requests to ensure understanding is happening. Either ask for a reflection or ask what comes up for your listener. Practice making requests for understanding as many times as possible today.

❧ 243 ❧
Intention for Self-responsibility

Today, hold the intention to be fully self-responsible. Express without blame. Connect your feelings to your needs. Make requests instead of expecting people to know what you want. Claim your opinions as opinions instead of facts.

✎ 244 ✎
Intention for Self-compassion

Intend to be compassionate toward yourself today. Make empathy guesses of yourself when feelings arise. Give yourself encouragement and understanding. Give yourself three small self-connection breaks during the day. Pause. Breathe deeply. Check in on your sensations, feelings, and needs. Breathe and allow with kindness.

✎ 245 ✎
Do Overs

Today if you interact in a way that is out of alignment with your NVC or with your values, ask for a do-over as soon as possible, even in the moment it slips out of your mouth if you can. Just make an honest expression and then share what you would have liked to say instead. Example: "Oh, I realize that the way I just said that may have been hard for you to receive and it was out of alignment with my value for respect. I'd like to try that again. Would you mind?" Do your best to express in your natural way using the elements of NVC.

✎ 246 ✎
Do Overs

Do overs can come later too. If you don't have the nerve or instant awareness to ask for a do-over right away, you can do it later when you are more ready. You can ask for a do-over with care for the other. Offer transparency about what you did not like, the needs you didn't meet and what you would like to be different to better meet needs.

Practice writing requests for do overs. Choose an interaction you wish you could do over. Practice what you would say when sharing your expression in NVC instead of how you did it the first time.

❧ 247 ❧
Paused Lately?

Today, take some time to slow down, especially when you get stimulated. Remember to create pauses when you need to self-connect, manage your nervous system, or take space for self-empathy. Note when you are triggered and use your pause phrase or create a new one. Here are some phrases you can adopt: "Hold on a moment, please." "I need to gather my thoughts for a minute." "This matters to me, I need a moment here." "I'll get right back to you on that within (amount of time)." "I feel a bit overwhelmed. I'd like a moment please."

❧ 248 ❧
Bug in the Ear

Sometimes a listener's beliefs, past experiences, wounding, understanding of words, self-esteem, conditioning of any kind create a personal filter that distorts what they hear. I call that a bug in the ear. You may have a bug in your ear if you tend to hear communication from others as demands whether they intend so or not. In many cultures people are conditioned to think we are required to respond to others immediately even when there is no actual urgent situation or emergency. We experience much stress due to receiving this demand regularly. The result may be speaking before self-connection, speaking when triggered, saying yes when we mean no, and more. Notice today whether you are responding with awareness and self-connection or from a mindset of I *must* respond now.

❧ 249 ❧
Bug in the Ear

Consider for a moment that everyone has a bug in the ear. Everyone has conditioning, beliefs, wounding, past experiences that influence present interpretation, and a different way of seeing things. The opportunity here is to know this and to act as if the bug is active all the time. Let it serve as a reminder to check for understanding whenever you express something that matters to you because the bug has likely stirred things around, so the listener may have heard something different from what you intended. Today practice making connection requests to find out whether your listeners are hearing what is important to you.

❧ 250 ❧
Bug in Your Ear

You also have a bug in your ear. Everything someone says has to go through your bug or filter! Don't assume you understand someone as they intended you to understand. Check it out! They may not ask you for a reflection or a check. You can offer this to confirm you have clearly and accurately received the message they sent. Today, practice making reflections in question form. Examples: "Is it that you are anxious and want to ensure that the procedure is clearly laid out and followed?" "Are you excited when you think about the upcoming event because the sense of connection and fun is so important to you?" "Is it that you are concerned because it is important to you to contribute and you're not sure if what you are doing is as effective as you would like?"

Assuming

by Kathy Ziola

I know. I know. I know.
I am sure that I know
What should be going on,
Why you said what you said,
The right way to do this,
The way it really happened.
I know that I know!
And you should know that!

I'm sure you did that on purpose
Just to get me going,
Just to show how smart you are,
Just to manipulate
the situation to your favor.
I'm sure I don't matter here.
I am sure that I'm sure!
And you should know that for sure!

No room for two of us
No room for both our views
No room for other possibilities
No room for real connection
When we think we know it all
When we know that we are right
When we think we know what's true.
Curiosity is the way out of assumption.
Let's assume I'm right...
but just about this!

❧ 251 ❧
Bug in the Ear

A particular bug that can cause trouble is one I call the assumption bug! That is one that is tough to get past and may completely block your hearing! If you assume you already know what someone thinks, feels, wants, or values, or if you assume you know how they will respond to something, you may be way off. You may act as if your assumption is true and not see or hear the person before you. This can be extremely frustrating for them and for you. Today, check yourself for assumptions. Write down all forms of assumptions you notice today. These may be obvious or more subtle. Pay extra close attention. Examples of assumptions that may impact your behavior or words:

> My partner always....
>
> The other person intends to make my life harder.
>
> The other person is just thinking of themselves.
>
> I know what they really mean.
>
> I know what is going on with them.
>
> I know better than they do.
>
> I know what their intentions are.

❧ 252 ❧
Assumption

After having noticed your assumptions yesterday, today you can become curious instead. When an assumption comes to mind today, pause and question its validity. Ask yourself if you can know it to be true for sure. Practice checking out your assumption before acting upon it or speaking based on it. Try asking for more information and clarification about what is going on, what the intentions are, etc., instead of behaving as if your assumption is true.

∽ 253 ∾
Remembering Compassion

Take five to ten minutes today to sit quietly and think about your intention for bringing compassion into your interactions. Consider why compassion is important to you in relating. What do you like about it? What does it feel like to feel compassion? How does compassion live in and through you in conversation? Ask this question of yourself before and during each interaction today: "How can I bring compassion forward now?" Write about your experiences at the end of the day.

∽ 254 ∾
Remembering Empathy

Remember a time when you received empathy and care from someone when you needed it. Take a few moments now to recall this experience fully. Feel the warmth of that understanding and care. Let yourself remember the satisfaction and connection. Relish this for at least one minute. Let it nourish you now again. This practice impacts your brain and nervous system, encouraging and building pathways of positivity, healing the brain and heart from times of lack of empathy.

೫ 255 ೫

Remembering Beautiful Needs

With all the fullness of life's challenges and busyness, it can be easy to lose touch with our deeper values and yearnings. Managing and doing what needs to be done each day can be overwhelming in that we just move from doing to more doing, and the aspect of simply being is lost to our awareness. Today, set an alarm or timer to stop at least three times throughout the day to pause, breathe, and remember one beautiful need/value/quality of life that you care about. Relish its beauty and unique contributions to life for a few moments. Envision how you can bring that energy into whatever you are doing next. It can be a simple holding of it in your heart, doing actions with the energy of that need, or even speaking it or using it more overtly in your conversation or activity.

೫ 256 ೫

Remembering

Spend some time now to remember what it is that draws you to NVC. What is the impact on your life of using NVC? How has managing to recall one component or one principle in each moment had an effect? What have you noticed? What is the most important part of NVC for you right now? Take time to contemplate and write a bit about this.

❧ 257 ❧

Just Get It Done

Sometimes we just need to get it done. We just need the child to get dressed and out the door. We just need to accomplish the goals by the deadline. We just need to be prepared for that meeting. There are situations where the just-get-it-done approach becomes necessary due to the setting, commitments to others, time constraints, or responsibilities. It can be difficult to imagine using NVC in these situations. Yet there can be a cost to that in the long run. Damage to relationships may result. Today, pay attention to the just-get-it-done attitude you may see in yourself or others. Notice the impact on you and others. Notice the short-term impact and imagine or notice the possible long-term ramifications. Write a bit about this.

❧ 258 ❧

Just Get It Done

When the just-get-it-done energy comes up today, notice any demand energy and any energy of urgency. Take a moment for a reality check with yourself and any others involved. Is it truly urgent? Can you make it a true request? Can you hear a request instead of a demand? Are you just fine with the get it done approach in the situation? Are you connected to the needs behind the feeling in the moment? Is there a sense of alignment or agreement that feels good, or are you or others feeling resentment, stress, or frustration? Do you believe there is only one way to approach the situation or task? Can you be open to other possibilities? Could you have a needs-based conversation in the moment or perhaps later after the goal is attained? Are you maintaining connection in the midst of just getting it done? What difference would that make?

❧ 259 ❧
Gain Listening

When you have something important to say and want to make sure you get heard, you can do several things to ensure the best possibility of being heard the way you hope. Try one or more of these today: Make sure you have the person's full attention before speaking. Use their name and tell them you would like to talk about something important. Make sure the person has time, availability, and capacity to listen at the moment. Before expressing, let the person know that it is important to you, and you would like a reflection to make sure you have expressed yourself clearly. If you don't ask for reflection in advance, ask for it after you share.

❧ 260 ❧
Immediacy

Immediacy is the practice of speaking what is present in the moment. Instead of talking around an issue or disconnecting when you don't know what to say or do, you can speak to the process at the very moment. Examples: "I am so surprised by what I hear you saying, and I need a moment to let it sink in so I can understand." "When I think about our situation, I am at a loss. I'd like to just sit a moment to get clarity and ponder what to do next." "I want to talk about something important, and I am really nervous because our relationship is so important to me, and I want to do this in a way that works for both of us. Are you open to just listening while I try to get this out?" Try some immediacy today. Say what is present in the moment using the NVC elements of observation, feeling, need, request.

❧ 261 ❧
Positive Empathy

Empathy is not only for the challenges in life. It is also a deep response of companionship in the positive experiences of life. When someone shares excitement and celebration of something wonderful, give an empathic reflection. You may have a habit of stating an evaluation, saying how you feel about it, or sharing a similar experience of your own. This can take the joy out of it for the person sharing and shift the spotlight to you or the evaluation. Try reflecting what you hear the person is really enjoying, what their feeling is, and the needs that are being satisfied. This opens the door for them to share even more of what they are enjoying as you give companionship. Make it all about them before sharing your feelings, stories, opinions, or approval.

❧ 262 ❧
Share Your Joy

We tend to want to celebrate accomplishments, excitements, inspirations, pleasant experiences, milestones, and so much more. NVC is a tool for deepening companionship in celebrations and acknowledgments. Dive in! Go ahead and enjoy deeply with others. Acknowledge and celebrate the joys of life. Let's turn it around this time. Find something you are pleased with today and share it with a friend. Ask them for a reflection of what they hear is important and wonderful for you.

Reconnecting After Conflict

I cherish the NVC skills I've learned over time, especially the art of reconciliation after a disagreement. One day, while visiting my parents, my father and I had a tense exchange. He wanted me to do something, but I couldn't understand what it was. Frustration built up, and I ended up snapping at him, saying, "Why couldn't you just ask me directly instead of using so many words?" I stormed off, feeling angry and regretful. Our relationship means a lot to me, and I craved compassion and peace in our interactions.

After taking thirty minutes to calm down, I practiced NVC self-empathy. I acknowledged my feelings, listened to my judgments with compassion, and explored the needs behind my emotions. I realized that I was frustrated, yearning for understanding and ease in communicating with my father. Regret washed over me for snapping, knowing how much I valued our connection.

Feeling calmer, I approached my father to engage in NVC reconciliation. I shared my regrets about my behavior and expressed that his feelings mattered to me. I asked him how he felt during our exchange and listened attentively as he shared his emotions. Using empathic questions, I reflected to him what I heard, seeking to truly understand his perspective.

Afterward, I asked if he would be open to hearing how the situation affected me. He listened with empathy, understanding my feelings and needs. Together, we brainstormed strategies for better communication and mutual care in the future.

Thanks to NVC, our conversation transformed into a moment of healing, understanding, and connection. Looking back, I'm incredibly grateful for these skills. In the past, I might have blamed my father or kept my feelings to myself, harboring resentment. NVC has shown me a different path, one that fosters empathy, compassion, and genuine connection. Ahhh!

Jessica Cinco, Global Educator, Course Instructor, Teach English Now! Arizona State University

❧ 263 ❧
Back to Basics - Motivation

Focus today on recognizing that everything anyone says or does is an attempt to meet a beautiful, universal need. Be curious about what needs may be motivating all those words and actions that you hear and see. Notice how you feel when you do this.

❧ 264 ❧
Back to Basics - Observation

Pay attention today to any tendency to judge others that may pop up for you. Notice how you feel when judgments arise. Pause, and translate the judgments into clear observations. Notice how you feel when you do this.

∞ 265 ∞

Back to Basics - Needs

Pay attention today to any tendency to judge others that may pop up for you again. Notice how you feel when judgments arise. Pause, and translate the judgments into needs. Notice how you feel when you consider the deeper needs versus focusing on and believing judgments.

∞ 266 ∞

Back to Basics - Request

When you make a request today, check in with the other person to see whether they hear any demand in what you are asking. If so, ask for a do-over. Then take a moment to self-connect and then express from a more open frame of mind and heart.

∞ 267 ∞

Back to Basics - Feelings

Pay attention to whether you are putting responsibility for your feelings outside yourself. You may hear or think things such as, "That made me feel _____." "You made me feel _____." "He (she, it, they) make me feel _____." "You need to _____ so I can feel _____." See if you can connect your feelings to your needs instead. "When I see/hear _____ I feel _____ because ____ (need) ____ is important to me."

❧ 268 ❧
Back to Basics

"How can I make life more wonderful?" is a key question that Marshall Rosenberg used in his living and teaching of NVC. Use this question as your inquiry today and see where it leads you. Write about your experience.

❧ 269 ❧
Abundance

When we are attached to a position, an outcome, or a particular strategy, we are in a mindset of limitation and lack. We may think there is only one way, or I can only be happy if this happens or this person responds the way I want. When we shift into a mindset of abundance, we can loosen our grip on such positions and attachments and trust that there are numerous ways to meet the needs at hand. Today, practice thinking of at least three strategies to meet any need that comes up. Have fun stepping into abundance and creativity!

❧ 270 ❧
Abundance

When we can truly connect with one another and get some synergy going, we often find more possible strategies than we imagined. Try playing the Highest Thought Game. This is where you discover all the needs and then generate as many ideas as possible to meet as many needs as possible. Let go of attachment to who thinks of what and go with the highest thought. Go with the idea that meets the most needs with the most aliveness and enjoy! Try this out today with any situation needing some resolution or strategizing. No matter how small of a situation, try it for practice and fun.

∞ 271 ∞
Control as a Strategy

Sometimes control is expressed as a need. I think of it as a strategy to meet needs. There are often some powerful urges for control that stem from needs for safety and security based on the past. These needs or others may come into play for you. Take some time today to contemplate, inquire, and write about your relationship to control as a strategy. Use these questions to explore: How do you feel when others try to control you? In what situations do you most often use control? What needs do you attempt to meet by taking control of a situation? What needs are you trying to meet by controlling others' behaviors? What needs do you meet by controlling yourself? How have you used control to serve you?

∞ 272 ∞
Control and Self-empathy

Spend some time in self-empathy today for yourself and your beautiful needs related to the strategy of control. Speak to yourself with kind understanding and encouragement. Reflect and be with any pain or mourning arising from these needs and any related early experiences.

❧ 273 ❧
Control and Impact

Having explored your relationship to control and what needs you try
to meet, now explore how your strategy of controlling impacts others.
Ask yourself what reactions to your control you have noticed others
have. Do some writing about this. If you want to really stretch, ask
someone you trust if, for the sake of learning, they would be willing to
share how it impacts them when you use control to meet your needs.
You will want to be ready with some empathy and reflection for them
if you make this request. Journal your experience and what you learn.

❧ 274 ❧
Control

Spend some time today in self-empathy about your relationship to
control and the impact on others. Bring some compassion to yourself
for your efforts to meet your needs in ways that sometimes work well
and sometimes not so much. Meet any feelings and needs that arise
with loving kindness and understanding.

❧ 275 ❧
Control

Consider whether there is someone with whom you have used control
to power over them where you met your needs at their expense and
would now like to heal the interaction. Spend some time in self-
connection to prepare for a healing conversation. Take responsibility
for your choices and strategies. Consider the needs and feelings of
the other. Prepare to listen to them and offer empathy and express
your regrets. You can practice doing it live tomorrow.

I Blew It

by Kathy Ziola

Holy smoke I didn't mean it!
I lost my cool just for a minute.
The damage is done and you're in pain.
I feel so rotten once again.
Bricks of pain start to create
A wall of resentment that separates

This time I've done it I'm pretty sure
It's gonna be tough to find the cure.
Could we take some time to hash this out?
Tell me now what your pain is about.
I'll listen with care and empathy impart.
This impact on you is breaking my heart.

I want to express my deep regret.
You matter to me, please don't forget.
Could we have a 'do-over' please?
I know I can do better, I'm on my knees
Vulnerable, humble, learning the way
I'd like to grow and live compassion today.

∞ 276 ∞
Healing Conversation

Invite the person with whom you were controlling to have a conversation for healing. Share the basic topic that you would like to discuss and gain their agreement to have the conversation. Ask them to share the impact of your control actions and any feelings they may have. Invite them to share what matters to them. Offer loads of empathy. Let them know how they matter to you and how your actions did not meet the need for care for them or other related needs that matter to you. If they are open, share what was going on for you and what needs you were trying to meet by using control. Risk some vulnerability. Share what you wish you had done instead. Ask for some reflection. Ask how it is for them to hear. Make space for anything else that needs to be shared.

∞ 277 ∞
Control

Today, explore what strategies besides controlling people or situations you could use to meet needs. Choose some specific needs you have previously tried to meet using control and find new ways to meet those particular needs.

❧ 278 ❧
Immediacy

Staying with what is really present is the practice today. In addition to the initial quality of immediacy that you bring to the opening of a conversation, practice staying in the conversation from moment to moment by expressing honestly what is present now. And now. And now. When someone says "No" to a request you make, for instance, that isn't necessarily the end of the conversation. Say what is real for you next. Get curious. Ask them to share what is real for them in the moment. If someone objects or rejects what you are expressing on a topic, stay present and share what is now coming up for you. Moment to moment, say what is alive with responsibility and clarity of feelings and needs.

❧ 279 ❧
Broom and Dustpan

Sometimes we make a mess of things when communicating. Thankfully we have NVC to clean up after ourselves. If you have something you have said or done that you think contributed to a communication mess, pull out your NVC clean-up tools and get started. First, employ self-empathy, then invite the others into conversation to clean up any misunderstandings, hear about impact, express your regrets, and mourn together to reconcile. Don't sweep the mess under the rug!

❧ 280 ❧
Simplicity

Today, try using this simple inquiry in any situation: What is at the heart of the matter? Then respond from your heart, whether that is with empathy, honesty, or self-empathy.

❧ 281 ❧
Self-check

Today, simply check in once per hour to notice and allow your feelings and needs. Set an alarm so that you can pause for thirty seconds to one minute each hour and be present to yourself compassionately this way.

Empathy & Empowerment

My daughter was in sixth or seventh grade. It was Sunday night at about 9:15. She was sitting at the computer trying to get her homework done for Monday morning. I had gone into the room to tell her it was bedtime and she said she had important work due in the morning. I might have said something to her like "You should have thought about that way before now. It's time for bed," or "When are you going to ever learn? I told you that you are supposed to get your homework done on Fridays so you don't have to worry about it the rest of the weekend. You did this to yourself." Instead, I took a breath and remembered to give some empathy. I asked her how she was doing with it. She told me she was so tired and frustrated and that her work was important to her, and she wanted to do a good job because her schoolwork really mattered to her. I reflected with some gentle empathy and said, "Are you just so tired and frustrated right now because you are torn between sleep and doing your homework because you want to be successful and do a good job?" She said yes and expressed how hard it was to try to do it at the last minute on Sunday night when she was so exhausted. I reflected, "Is it just so hard to do your assignment when you are this tired?" She said yes and that she was really bummed she had waited so late. I asked if she was disappointed because it matters to her to be able to be good in school and also enjoy her weekend. She expressed that she wished she had done it on Friday because this really didn't feel good. She decided for herself to do her homework on Fridays or Saturday mornings from now on so she could avoid this situation again and be able to really enjoy her weekends. And she did just that from then on. She found her own wisdom and made her own decision. Had I scolded her, tried to control her, and told her she had to do her homework on Fridays from now on we would have been in a weekly power struggle. As it was, she learned, was empowered, and took responsibility for her own values, for doing her work, and being successful.

∽ 282 ∽
Simply Empathy

Imagine you have just plastered *empathy* across the inside of your eyes so you can always see it. Let it remind you to first offer empathy today as many times as you can do so. Be sure to make empathetic reflections that focus on what the person values/needs vs the unmetness of the needs.

Example: "Is it that you are frustrated because you value understanding?" vs "Is it that you are frustrated because your need for understanding is not being met?"

❦ 283 ❧

Simplicity

Today, focus on the understanding that everyone is trying to meet a beautiful, universal human need through whatever words or actions they use. Allow this to open your heart to compassion and curiosity about what needs are present in any given situation.

❦ 284 ❧

Body Empathy

Today, simply notice your body sensations and give some love to yourself as you experience them. Give a gentle kind of empathy and care for whatever your body experiences today. You can talk inwardly to your body as if it were a friend to whom you want to give comfort, acknowledgment, and empathy. Explore how this can sound and feel.

Example: "Hello back. I notice you are hurting today. Is it that you have been straining lately and really want some rest? I want you to know that I hear your message. You have been working hard, and I want you to know that I appreciate you. I am going to take good care of you today."

❦ 285 ❧

Being Conscious

Feelings come and go. Let them come and let them move through. It is not necessary to attach to feelings and identify them as yourself. You are the one experiencing them. Notice how emotions have come and gone for years. They are impermanent. Notice your conscious self, the one who is having the experience. That constant one who notices is you. Simply notice and allow yourself to be okay as feelings come and go.

❧ 286 ❧

Love

Take a few moments to tap into the quality of life called love. Breathe deeply into your heart space. Let your chest and heart area expand. Focus on love. Remember a loving relationship or interaction. Think of someone you love. Notice what love feels like. Let it fill you up. Breathe love in and breathe love out as you move through your day. Imagine breathing love into your words today. Take a breath of love before you say each thing you say today. Speaking takes breath. Let it be a breath of love in and a breath of love that comes out in the form of your words. Write about your experience today.

❧ 287 ❧

Love

What do you love? Spend a little time sitting with and writing about what you love. What do you love to do, to be, to experience, to enjoy, to give, to receive, to share, to create, to contribute, to accomplish? What do you love? Let love fill your mind and heart today as you appreciate your experiences and the people you engage with. Focus on what you love and see how you feel and what needs you notice being met as you do this throughout your day. Capture your insights in your journal.

❧ 288 ❧

Love

Sit quietly now for a time. Settle into your breath and feel your body. Allow yourself to be here fully present with what is here with compassion and gentle kindness. Then, gently breathe into the heart space and tenderly envision your heart being soft, open, and expansive. Imagine it now with ears to hear all expressions through the heart of love. Imagine your heart with eyes to see all that happens through the filter of love. Imagine your heart with a mouth to speak words of love and care, compassion, and understanding. Let your experiences today process through the heart of love. Let your heart of love be the power with which you see, hear, and speak. Let the mind rest awhile as the heart takes charge. Capture your experience with this today in your journal.

❧ 289 ❧

Resistance

When you receive resistance from anyone today, pause and breathe into your heart. Take a moment to reframe judgments about resistance into curiosity about the needs this person is protecting or trying to meet. What fear may be present? Do they need to be heard and understood with some empathy? Do they need to understand you better? Were you clear and self-responsible with your expression? Are you making demands instead of requests? What can you invite them to consider in terms of needs? Don't fight resistance. Soften into it and be present with the person and the experience, bringing your compassion and curiosity. Journal about the impact of doing this today.

❧ 290 ❧
Resistance

Notice when resistance arises for you today. What needs might you be trying to protect or meet by resisting? Are you making a demand of yourself? Are you connected to the needs you would meet by doing what you are asking of yourself? Are you connected to your heart and the life energy that is moving in you? Are you fighting against a fear? Try taking some time to sit quietly with what is present in you that has brought up the resistance. Bring some gentle and kind understanding to the part of you that is resisting. You can even talk with it as you would with a friend. Ask your resistance to express. Listen to its needs. Offer empathy. Be curious and compassionate. Listen. Inner NVC dialogue can bring clarity and comfort and peace. Try it out today.

❧ 291 ❧
Why?

Asking why can sometimes bring clarity about someone's thinking that led to an action. It can bring understanding about a choice that was made. On the other hand, asking why can sometimes be a hindrance to forward movement. It can provoke defensiveness and conflict. Sometimes, things just happen, seemingly without a clear purpose or reason. Sometimes, people act without connection to all the needs and impacts. Asking "why me" can lead to suffering because taking the randomness of life personally can stimulate more pain on top of an already painful situation. Instead of asking why today, try asking what. What matters here? What do I value and feel? What do others value and feel? What needs were each of us trying to meet in the situation? What would I like to see happen to meet more needs? What can I do to contribute to things being better?

∽ 292 ∽
When?

When do you want to live your deepest values? What are you waiting for? What are you afraid of experiencing if you speak up or act in accordance with your values? Do some journaling today to explore what holds you back from being your truest self in this moment. When will you be and do and express all that you are? When are you waiting for? Could it be now? What would it be like to let yourself be fully you now? What would you do now? What would you say now? What would you create now? What would you stop doing or saying now? Often, we wait and hold back for fear of others' responses. It is usually due to lack of confidence in skills to navigate the conversations that may come. Use your NVC to express your true nature today. If you express and fear someone's reaction, be ready with empathy to hear and understand them. Be ready to share honestly what comes next for you. You have been practicing for many months now. If you use your skills, your love, and your heart, you can be confident in living your deepest values now. Now is when!

❧ 293 ❧
How?

Well, NVC offers us a lot of how. It is a model, a practice, a consciousness that helps us with how to communicate, how to connect, how to deepen intimacy, how to navigate conflict, how to enjoy and acknowledge and celebrate more fully. Today, go ahead and put some attention on the *how* of NVC. Recall and use basic templates for expression, empathy, and self-empathy. How matters. How do you want to relate today? Consider a conversation you will have today and think ahead to *how* to do it in NVC. It is okay to rely on the structure of *how to*, particularly when faced with a difficult conversation. That is the time to pull out the tools of how to connect because it is hard when you are stimulated or in the heat of a moment. Let the how of NVC be your foundation today. Write a bit about how this impacts you today.

❧ 294 ❧
Who?

Who will you interact with today? Who are they to you? How will you live your values as you meet them, interact with them, serve them, collaborate with them? Who do you want to be as you interact? Who are you in your day? Who are you to others? How will you impact them? Who do you want to be in their memories? Journal this inquiry if you like. Then take the highest intentions of your who exploration into your day.

❧ 295 ❧
Fairness

Somehow some of us have gotten the idea that things should be fair. I invite you to check into your sense of fairness. Are you attached to this idea? How do you feel when you think something is unfair? Have a look underneath the idea of fairness and see what needs are related to it. Is it that you want to know that you or someone you care about matters? Is it that you want equal care for needs? Is it that you want full expression, shared resources, opportunities for everyone, acknowledgment? I invite you to explore beneath fairness and your attachment to it. There may be strategies that meet needs in wonderful ways and yet do not fit the definition of fair.

❧ 296 ❧
Respect

Today, notice how the need for respect lives in you. Do you want it from others? Do you value it more from some people than others? Who? What happens to you when you think someone does not respect you? How have you tried to gain others' respect in ways that feel inauthentic? Journal about this inquiry today.

❧ 297 ❧
Respect

Respect is a need that may be either internally or externally focused. When we name the need for respect in conversation, it can come across as stating that the other does not hold respect. This may or may not be true and may stimulate defensiveness. Check underneath the need for respect. You can do this using your needs list and asking, "If I had respect what would that give me?" or "If I had respect, what other needs would be met?" Is there another layer of needs that is present? These needs may be more vulnerable and easier for others to hear.

❧ 298 ❧

The Beauty of Respect

Consider the quality we call respect. Sit quietly and notice its unique energy and beauty. Let respect fill your whole being. During the day today, each time before you speak, bring that experience of respect back up and speak with that energy imbuing your words and body language.

❧ 299 ❧

Express Respect

Today, practice living respect again by expressing authentically to someone you hold respect for. Let them know that you respect them, sharing how they matter to you and how you appreciate them.

✑ 300 ✑
Respecting Differences

Today, notice whether you respect some people or types of people more or less than others. Notice what it is that contributes to any difference for you. Do you notice biases or evaluative thoughts that contribute to this in you? These might include beliefs about whether someone deserves respect based on their behaviors, position of authority, age, gender, intelligence, race, education, job or career, place of residence, family history, amount of wealth, accent, rate of speech, etc. Consider the impact of how this feels to you. Do you treat people differently based on your ideas of respect or who deserves more or less respect? Is this congruent with other beautiful needs you hold precious?

✑ 301 ✑
Self-Respect

Today, practice holding respect for yourself. Before expressing yourself, take a moment to internally remember these ideas: My needs matter. I have something to contribute. I am doing my best here. I respect myself. My unique ways of thinking, feeling and expressing are valid. I am learning, growing, and being fully human.

✑ 302 ✑
Encouragement

Today, use an NVC expression to encourage one or more people. Share your confidence in their ability or acknowledge something you see and appreciate about them as a person, or give appreciation for their efforts. Examples: "I have seen you set goals and accomplish them. I feel confident you will find your way through this challenge too." "When I hear you talk about your commitment to your relationship, I feel inspired by the love and effort that you contribute, and it gives me a different perspective on life."

∞ 303 ∞
Speaking Up

Today, practice saying at least one thing that you feel shy or hesitant to say. It may be a need you want to express, an acknowledgment, or a bit of empathy to someone who needs it. Practice speaking up authentically using the components of NVC in a way that feels natural to you.

∞ 304 ∞
Speak Up with Confidence

Look for an opportunity to contribute something unique today, whether at work or in a personal relationship. You have a perspective, an opinion, a creative idea, some feedback, or a bit of encouragement to share. Trust yourself to add value to life today! Use your NVC honest expression components to share without judgment or demand. Own your expression and offer it with the energy of a gift. Ask how it lands for your listeners.

I'm Listening

by Kathy Ziola

I'm listening
I am listening with my soul
Yes, I'm listening
I am listening to your soul

Just for once, Just this moment
Just this now. Like the first
Time I ever heard you speak
Like this moment is all there is

As I let go of my thoughts
I am hear just as I am
As I rest here with you
Just as you are
I let go of everything and let you be
Just let you be

And in the space that's in between us
Filling and enfolding us, there is love, sweet love.
Compassion calls us home
Home to tenderness
Home to just listening
With our souls

And when we speak, when we move
It is the power of Presence that brings us home
Home to the truth
Just listening

✑ 305 ✑
Empathy

Focus on empathy today. Remember that empathic reflections can be given for positive and challenging experiences. Capture the essence of what is shared and reflect feelings and needs as a question to see whether you have understood accurately. Examples: "Are you so excited about your trip because you love the learning and inspiration that comes from adventure?" "Is it that you are feeling deeply satisfied after talking to your daughter because your connection with her and your ability to support her are so important to you?" "Are you frustrated and overwhelmed right now because efficiency matters to you, and you just don't know how you will get it all done?" "Is it because care and well-being matter so much to you that you are angry and scared when you see how the nursing staff has made mistakes with your dad's medication?"

Be sure to make it a question instead of a statement like "You are…," or "It sounds like you…." These are evaluations instead of questions and may stimulate defensiveness if you aren't accurate.

✑ 306 ✑
Holding All Needs with Care

Think about something in your day today that you really want/ed to go well or be a certain way. Maybe it's a way you want/ed someone to respond, or something you want/ed to do. Notice how it feels to hold this outcome or strategy with that desire. What feelings come up for you related to this? Pressure, urgency, disappointment, excitement, joy, resistance, fear, desperation, or…? Notice and be compassionately present to this experience. Now notice the needs you want/ed to meet. Are there other strategies, outcomes, or responses you would be open to or even enjoy?

Now consider the needs of any others in the situation. Put yourself in their place and explore the feelings and passionately held needs they may have. Recall the principle of holding everyone's needs with care. How does this awareness affect your sense of attachment to outcomes?

❧ 307 ❧
Sweet Pain

Today when you notice any unmet needs, I invite you to bring your tender self-empathy into play. Allow the longing or mourning to be here just as it is. Giving it space and understanding and a gentle presence allows it to unwind. Notice how this feels and the sweetness of just accepting and allowing feelings and needs. When you notice a shift, gently call into your heart the beauty of the needs you so value. See if you can hold the pain and the sweetness of compassion and allow life to have its way with you all at once. It's a kind of sweet pain that seems to be an appreciation of the very aliveness of life as it is.

❧ 308 ❧
Suffering

Being human involves experiencing pain. We all have pain! Suffering is another thing. I mean suffering as the mental/emotional aspect of how we relate to pain. Suffering can come from thinking that something should or should not be a certain way. Such resistance to what is tends to create suffering in the forms of anger, conflict, or resentment. Today, look for any instance where you notice that your 'should thinking' is creating suffering in you. Take a few moments to notice your specific thoughts and listen to the needs contained within them. Journal this inquiry.

❧ 309 ❧
Trust

Today put some attention on trust as you interact. You can trust that people will be people with all the complexity of human nature, conditioning, capacities, and skills. You cannot necessarily trust people to do or be how you want. You can learn to trust that you can choose your responses consciously and that your intentions are positive as you grow in your communication skills. Explore in your journal today. What do I know and trust about myself? What skills do I have that I trust myself to use in communicating? What do I trust about the people I interact with the most? How do I build trust in my relationships? If you are up for it, have a conversation about trust with someone you would like to share more trust with. This is a topic for practicing conversation using expression, empathic listening, and self-connection. You could use any universal need as an NVC discussion for interesting practice. Example opening to a conversation about trust: "I value our relationship and am interested in exploring the topic of trust together for fun and the possibility of growth and learning. Are you open to talking a bit about what trust means to each of us and what that might look like in our relationship?"

❧ 310 ❧

Decision-Making

Remember today the key NVC key principle of taking responsibility for our actions. This means connecting to the needs behind any choices we may make. Connecting to the needs in a heartfelt way can assist in making decisions. Today, focus on knowing what needs are motivating you before you decide to take any action. Capture your exploration of your decisions and the related needs in your journal.

❧ 311 ❧

Decision-Making

Consider a decision you have made or one you need to make. Lay out your options and sit with each one. In this sitting, explore the needs you would meet with each choice and the needs you may not meet with each choice. Then sit quietly, imagine each option, and notice the energy you feel in your body and heart. Notice which option attracts you and increases energy or sense of peace, calm, or enthusiasm.

❧ 312 ❧

Pulling Ears

Sometimes being heard the way we would like is difficult. The other person may simply not understand, may feel defensive, have a hard time receiving feedback or new ideas, or be triggered by a past experience, to name a few. Patience, empathy, and repetition may be helpful in these cases. Try using a bit of persistence today to make sure you are heard and understood. Use your connection requests to check and see what the listener has heard before moving on. This is a bit like gently tugging on the listener's ears to see if they are hearing and understanding you.

❧ 313 ❧
Pulling Ears

Another technique for pulling on the ears of a listener may be to interrupt and make another request. For example, if you express and ask for a reflection and they start talking about their own response instead, you can say "Would you please hold on a moment? I'd like to make sure what I have said has come across clearly before we move ahead. Would you be willing to tell me what you heard before sharing more, please?" Practice pulling on a few ears today to make sure clarity is attained.

❧ 314 ❧
Is It Working?

Your perception of whether NVC is working can depend on your personal concept of the right outcome for your communication. Some people consider NVC as working if their request is met, or their strategy accepted. That is one way of thinking about it. I would suggest that NVC may also be working even if that is not the case. When you use your NVC today, pay attention primarily to the quality of connection and understanding that is taking place versus any particular outcome or agreeing with someone. Can you notice connection even when differences are present?

❧ 315 ❧
Is It Working?

Pay attention to your inner experience of NVC today. Let the idea of NVC working be related to your sense of self-awareness. Are you connected to your feelings, your needs, your observations? Are you using NVC to give yourself compassion? Are you using it to hold compassion for others in your mind and heart? Notice how NVC is working inside you today. Are you working NVC?

❧ 316 ❧
Letting Go

If you have a relationship in which you feel hopeless to connect in the way you would like, you may think, NVC *isn't working.* Suppose you are attached to a person responding in a particular way or a relationship going a certain way and are using NVC to try to make that happen. In that case, it may be that NVC is not bringing that particular result. It may be that the other person does not actually have the commitment, the willingness, or the mental or emotional capacity to engage in the way your heart desires. Using NVC to the best of your ability will serve you in being in integrity with your values and will provide the best possibility for connection. And sometimes connection just isn't available. Using NVC and doing your best to connect will provide information on whether connection is possible. Sometimes letting go is necessary. Letting go with compassion and understanding instead of anger and judgment is a gift to both parties. Using your journal, write about what comes up for you, how NVC is working for you, and what you might want to let go of.

Expand your capacity to meet life with open-hearted presence.

❧ 317 ❧
Capacity

Capacity is our ability to think, feel, respond, manage energy, relate, empathize, self-connect, see clearly, and meet and navigate challenges and changes in a given moment. "How is my capacity?" is an important question to ask as you enter conversations that are important. If you are hungry, tired, overwhelmed or needing empathy, this may not be the time to have that important conversation. Pay attention today to your level of energy and capacity for challenges. If your capacity is low, you may want to use your honest expression for a bit of transparency and let the person know you need time or space before that conversation. Be sure to express your care and let them know a specific time when you would like to return to the conversation with more energy and capacity. This allows them to relax and trust that it matters to you.

❧ 318 ❧
Capacity

Spend some time today inquiring into your capacity level in general. If you experience it as high, explore a bit what feeds you and keeps it that way so you can consciously maintain and enhance it. If you find you are often running at low capacity for challenges, spend some time inquiring into what is impacting you. What needs would you like to meet more fully to help you feel full of energy, willing and able to face challenging interactions? Rest, food, empathy, self-empathy, acceptance, creativity, support…other…?

❧ 319 ❧
Build Your Capacity

Having explored needs that support your capacity yesterday, create some strategies to meet those needs. Make concrete and doable requests of yourself and/or others to engage in the strategies. Be sure to include when, how, where, and how often you will do these things to build your capacity to engage in life and interactions fully. Put the plans in your calendar and treat them like important appointments.

❧ 320 ❧
Capacity - Nourish Yourself

Building the capacity to be present for interactions that may be challenging or just to be fully present to life and others can be done through self-empathy. Today, spend some time nourishing yourself through being present to your feelings and needs. Depending on others to give this to us works part of the time, and providing deep care and self-empathy increases energy, presence, availability to be there for others, and capacity to navigate difficulties.

✎ 321 ✎
Capacity and Empathy

If your empathy reservoir is empty, meaning your capacity for giving is low, you may just need some empathy and a bit of understanding and loving support yourself. Today, ask someone you feel comfortable with to just listen to you a bit and offer some reflections of what you are feeling and what they hear is important to you. They don't need to know NVC. You can ask them in a way that draws them into NVC-type empathy without getting concerned over details. Just asking as I suggested above can guide them to give you what you hope for.

✎ 322 ✎
Higher Connection & Essence

Today, when you enter a conversation, imagine that you are speaking directly to the other person's best version of themselves. Imagine you can see them at their very essence as an innocent being and doing their best in the moment. Imagine their essence being pure and clear and full of positive intentions. Just play with this today and see what happens within you and in the interactions. Express in your journal as always.

❧ 323 ❧

Higher Connection

Life is moving in and through you. Life is moving in and through everyone with whom you come into contact today. We all have thoughts, feelings, needs, desires, priorities, goals, and unique ways of expressing ourselves. This is life energy moving in and through each of us. Life is meeting life as you interact. Pay attention to this life in each one of you. You can notice it as actions, words, movements, feelings, longings, sensations, needs, and requests. NVC enables us to connect to life as it expresses uniquely in any moment. Journal about how you experience your connections to life energy today.

❧ 324 ❧

Compromise

Compromise can bring a variety of responses. It may bring you a sense of appreciation, equality, fairness, or mattering. It may also bring resentment and feeling as though you are sacrificing, which doesn't feel good. Compromise may bring a sense of both parties feeling unsatisfied or resentful as if it is a lose/lose experience, or a win/lose situation. Explore and write about any situation you currently have, or have had in the past, where you felt compromise was involved. What feelings and needs were present for you? What feelings and needs do you imagine present for the other person? How did the compromise work out? How did it impact your relationship?

⤞ 325 ⤝
Compromise

Considering the compromise situation you explored yesterday, imagine a different approach and frame of mind. Imagine focusing on the needs of each person and holding care for all the needs. Imagine you placed all the needs in a basket together on a table. Open your heart in compassion for the other person as well as yourself. Both of you, all of you, matter. Focus on the beauty of the needs you are holding together. Think of them as *our needs* instead of mine or yours. Notice if you feel more of a shift toward meeting needs rather than a sense of compromise or sacrifice. This is a subtle nuance. It is an energetic shift that may add joy as you choose. It is based upon being moved by beautiful needs instead of a sense of should or fairness or sacrificing for each other and keeping score. Write what comes up for you as you do this.

Compassion hangs sweetly on the vine of authentic expression.

∽ 326 ∽

Boundaries (Standing Up for Your Needs)

This is a term that describes a sense of defining clear limits to what words or behaviors you may accept or not accept to meet your needs for safety, well-being, space, comfort, or other needs/values you hold. Spend some time journaling today about your needs in relation to others relative to your body and physical space. Discover the needs that would lead you to disengage if not met, your deal-breakers. After doing so, write a few honest expressions in NVC to share your feelings and needs about one or more of these deal-breakers. I invite you to consider using the expression *standing up for your needs*. When doing this you can make requests from others that you are actually not willing to negotiate. While this may sound like a demand, it can also be a request because you are asking for willingness. They can choose to say yes or no. You then have information to decide how you'll respond next, including disengaging or leaving.

∽ 327 ∽

Standing Up for Your Needs

Spend some time today exploring and writing about some of your strong needs related to others in your work setting, or a setting where you are working with others. After doing so, write one or more honest expressions in NVC to share your feelings and needs about one or more of these needs. Remember, you can make requests of others that you are not willing to negotiate. It is still a request because you are asking for willingness. They can choose to say yes or no. It is then simply information for how you decide to respond next, including disengaging or leaving.

✄ 328 ✄
Standing Up for Your Needs

There are times when protective use of force comes into play. This is when you prioritize safety and well-being on any level, and you do what needs to be done to protect those involved. It is done without anger or punishment. Return to dialogue whenever possible to work toward agreements and meeting needs peacefully, if possible. Consider any times when you took strong action to maintain safety. Write about how you went about this. What needs were at play? Did you act with anger and punishment? Did you share your needs and feelings or make initial requests? How might you do it differently now using your NVC?

✄ 329 ✄
Willing to Be Moved?

Entering into dialogue with a strong attachment to a preference or opinion is a recipe for struggle and potentially conflict. Being willing to be moved off a position will contribute to an energy of discovery and collaboration. Today as you interact, pay attention to your attachment to your positions and opinions and strategies. In any given situation today, see if you can think of two or three other strategies that could meet the same needs.

❧ 330 ❧
Dependence

Today, notice how you depend on others to have some of your needs met. What needs must you rely upon others to meet? How comfortable are you with this dependence? What feelings arise in you related to this? How do you feel when others depend upon you? What judgments do you hold related to dependence? What positive thoughts do you hold related to dependence, if any? How is dependence important and functional?

❧ 331 ❧
Independence Exploration

Today, notice whether you experience independence. Journal and explore the following inquiries. Where in your life do you express independence? Where do you long for more independence? How do you feel related to experiencing and not experiencing independence? How do you feel about people you evaluate as independent? What meaning do you attach to yourself about being independent or not being independent? How is independence important and functional? How might it not be functional? Journal your exploration. Share about your discoveries to practice NVC conversation if you like.

❧ 332 ❧
Notice Interdependence

Interdependence is the recognition that we are social creatures who interact and rely upon one another to meet needs. This is natural and necessary for most of us who are not hermits. Engaging in the acts of giving and receiving so that needs are met among people is an expression of interdependence. Explore today how you can notice interdependence in your life. Are you comfortable with both giving and receiving, or only one or the other? In what areas are you very dependent or very independent? How do you feel when you consider that you may sometimes be dependent and other times independent?

❧ 333 ❧
Interdependence in Life

Spend a few quiet minutes today focusing on gratitude for how you are able to give something to life, people, your work, your community and for how life in all its expressions gives to you. Write a bit about how you give and what impact that has, as well as how others give to you and how that impacts you. Notice and write about the exchange of support and contributions that you experience. See if you can discern aspects of dependence and independence that comprise interdependence and the awareness of how there is a shared reliance on individuals and systems and how individuals and groups all matter in meeting needs. Notice the constant exchange that allows us to meet needs. Return to the focus on gratitude for this experience.

✁ 334 ✁
Interdependence in Relationships

Notice that every action has a natural consequence in the context of relationships. When we act to meet a need in a relationship, there will be an impact on someone else's needs being met or not being met. If you care about the other, then meeting one of your needs at the expense of another person's needs impacts them, which in turn affects how they are, which affects how they interact and how they feel and how you feel. There is no real acting alone in relationships because all actions do have an effect on the other. For example, you may meet your personal needs for being understood or for efficiency while not meeting the other person's needs for understanding or empathy. You may have at the same time not met several needs you hold that relate to the other person, like care or consideration for them, or inclusion. Contemplate and journal today about this level of interdependence in one of your relationships where there is some tension, conflict, or attachment to a particular strategy. How do you notice the above dynamic in your experience?

✁ 335 ✁
Self-responsibility

Notice a need today that you expect or strongly desire, or maybe want to demand that someone else meet. What things could you do to meet that need for yourself? If you cannot think of a way to meet it for yourself externally, sit with the need and tap into its unique energy and beauty. Notice how it contributes to life and how you hold it precious and valuable. Allow yourself to imagine the need present and available to you right now. Let the sheer energy of this life-quality fill you up and nourish you. Sit with this fullness and beauty, letting your need be met internally. Notice how this impacts your body, emotions, and mind. After meeting the need internally, does any action naturally arise for you to take as an expression of this life quality? It may or may not. It may feel complete, or there may be a natural flow of action.

∞ 336 ∞
Think Before You Speak

This is an underlying premise in NVC. Taking time to self-connect before sharing is key to self-responsible authenticity. Today, try actively pausing before speaking. Take a moment to see what is really going on inside. When a feeling arises, resist the urge to share it before finding out what need is active in you at the moment. Practice saying, "I'd like a moment to consider before I respond." Play with this today by saying it as many times as you can in context. Then use the pause to self-connect before responding.

Empathy brightens lives through true understanding.

✍ 337 ✍
Consider the Other

Continue the practice of creating pauses today. Allow a gap between someone's speech and your response. In that little gap, focus on what you heard is important to the other person. What did you hear they are feeling and needing and wanting? Give an empathic reflection before sharing your own thoughts or feelings about the topic.

✍ 338 ✍
I'm Hurting - Reactions

When you feel hurt, how do you react? Do you withdraw? Attack? Defend? Freeze up? Cry? Hold a grudge? Try to get revenge or get even? Explore through some journaling today your reactions when someone says or does something, and you feel hurt. Becoming aware of your reactions can help you make more conscious choices to respond in meeting needs.

✍ 339 ✍
I'm Hurting - Inquiry

Remember the underlying NVC assumptions that feelings arise from needs and the things others say and do are the stimulus not the cause? When you feel hurt, it is time to look at assumptions, interpretations, and judgments. I recommend you don't believe everything you think. Your thinking may be causing the hurt feeling. Interpreting the meaning or intention behind someone's actions can be a misunderstanding.

One antidote is to check out the intentions or meaning the other person is holding. Try making an honest expression with a request to understand them better. Example, "I notice I am having some interpretations about what you did that could lead to some pain if they were accurate. I'd like to check out what is behind your actions. Would you be willing to share what motivated you to do that?"

❧ 340 ❧
I'm Hurting - Expressing

If you tend to withdraw when feeling hurt, you can use that withdrawal for some self-empathy. Then come back and make an expression about your pain and the needs that are important to you, followed by a connection request to make sure you are understood. If you have pain with someone, try that process out today. Or you can try self-empathy and honest expression by writing about a painful past interaction.

❧ 341 ❧
I'm Hurting

If you tend to attack when you feel hurt, you may regret it later. Blaming, labeling, evaluating, shaming, etc., can certainly escalate disconnection and conflict. Then both of you are in pain. Try taking some long, slow deep breaths. Be transparent and state that you are stimulated and need a moment. Do some self-empathy before responding with an honest expression or an empathic reflection. Practice this today if it comes up or journal the process for a past experience.

❧ 342 ❧
Defensiveness in Others

Notice today when other people seem defensive. How does it impact how you feel in their presence? How does it impact how you respond to them? How do you notice other people responding to them when they are defensive? What needs do you think are underlying the defensiveness?

❧ 343 ❧
Defensiveness in You

Whenever you feel defensive today, either pause and take a mental note for later journaling or pause in the moment if time is available. Jot down what comes up for you. What are you defending? What is it you are protecting? What would it be like if you did not defend? What needs are underneath your defensiveness? Notice how your defensiveness impacts those with whom you are interacting.

❧ 344 ❧
Defensiveness Transformation

Think of a situation in which you feel or have felt defensive. What are you feeling vulnerable, fearful, insecure, or embarrassed about? What other feelings might you be protecting with your defense? What needs are connected to these feelings? Spend a few minutes allowing yourself to compassionately be with your feelings and needs in the situation. Breathe deeply, notice your body, and bring some tenderness to yourself for your vulnerability. Would you be willing to share your vulnerability instead of defensiveness? How might you express these using observations, feelings, needs, connection requests? Practice by writing it out, role playing with a trusted friend, or speaking your authentic expression to the other person involved.

❧ 345 ❧
Being Right Impact

Attachment to being right can be a form of defensiveness, a protection against feeling vulnerable.

What would it mean *to you* to not be right? What would it mean *about you* if you were perceived as not right about something? I am not referring to situations where exact correctness for safety reasons is at hand. I am referring to the kind of attachment to being right in general conversation, which leads to power struggles and escalation of conflict. Does your attachment to being right create disconnection in your interactions? Pay attention to this today and journal what comes up.

❧ 346 ❧
Shift Being Right

Today, practice letting others be right. Let go of correcting how people express or the content they are sharing. Shift into a curious state of mind and ask for clarification if needed. Try saying yes first and then adding to whatever is being shared. Examples: "Yes, I hear that your experience is...and...I have another experience around that, (or a different experience)." "Is it that your information on this is ....? I'd like to hear more about that." "Are you open to hearing a different perspective?" These responses can lead to exploration and connection instead of arguing or struggling over rightness.

Family Differences

In late 2019, the news of becoming grandparents filled us with joy, but as 2020 brought the pandemic, fear and differing perspectives divide our family. My daughter-in-law's clinical anxiety amplified concerns, leading her and my vaccinated sons to adopt strict safety measures, while my husband and I chose alternativ1e care and were hesitant about the vaccines for health reasons. Despite the tensions, we aimed to understand and respect each other's choices. We complied with isolation and mask-wearing to visit our grandson, while they honored our fears. In the spring of 2022, we contracted COVID-19 but relied on early treatments. I provided my daughter-in-law with information, supplements, and drugs for early treatment when they traveled to visit her family before getting vaccinated, allowing them to feel more secure during their trip.

By recognizing the dissonance in our perceived realities and choosing to align our behavior with their needs, we managed to navigate through this challenging period while keeping our relationship intact. This experience highlighted the importance of empathy, understanding, and respectful communication when dealing with differing beliefs and perspectives, especially during such a divisive time as the pandemic.
Joyce, Grateful for NVC

❧ 347 ❧
Defensiveness & Assumptions

Defensiveness may come from assuming someone's intentions or that they are thinking a particular thought toward you or about you. Pay attention today to any assumptions or interpretations you make about others' thinking or intentions. Ask what is going on before defending against something that may not even be happening. Example: "I am not sure I understand where you are coming from on this. Would you mind sharing a bit more about your thinking behind it?"

❧ 348 ❧
Being Human

Ahh, to be so very human with all these feelings and beautiful needs! Being human includes a huge expanse of both positive and negative experience. Self-judgment can arise as we face our everyday experiences, doing our best to meet needs and sometimes falling short, impacting others in ways we don't like, or making mistakes that are uncomfortable for our egos. Journal a bit today on being human and the thinking that arises for you around your human foibles and challenges. Notice the flavor of your inner dialogue. Are you judging yourself? Are you compassionate toward yourself? Do you have a strong inner critic? Can you also acknowledge successes, creativity, congruence with your values, accomplishments, positive characteristics? Try doing so now. It can be tempting to focus only on the shortcomings.

❧ 349 ❧
Being Human

In the awareness of how you have been thinking toward yourself in your humanness, notice that you have a wide variety of capacities, skills, feelings, needs, thoughts, conditioning. They are all part of being human. Focus today on being kind and generous toward yourself regarding any idea or experience you have of falling short of your best intentions. Give yourself some understanding and compassion like you would a good friend to whom you want to give encouragement and empathy. Example, "Oh, (insert your name), are you a bit frustrated or disappointed in how you handled that? Would you really have liked to bring your values for _____ forward more fully?" Place your hand on your heart and bring some love and care for yourself and your experience. Give yourself a break. Cut yourself some slack. Notice your beautiful needs/values and how you want to bring them forward next time.

❧ 350 ❧
Humanness of Others

Put some conscious attention on others' humanity today. As you look at someone, consider what challenges they may be facing. Consider what feelings and needs might be present for them in something they are doing, whether meeting needs or not, whether that is in a work role, a personal interaction, or a social setting. Notice their humanity and practice holding compassion for their experience. Journal on what comes up when you do this about several people today.

✆ 351 ✆

Humanness of Others

Today, consider one or two people with whom you relate regularly. Reflect and write on the following inquiry. What do you notice about their humanness, their uniqueness, strengths, and vulnerabilities? What characteristics do they share with all human beings? What do you notice about your expectations of them? Do you expect them to be perfect or do things perfectly? Do you expect them to meet all your needs in just the ways you want? Do you get angry or disappointed when they do not? Do you tend to let them know what your needs are and make requests of them? How could you honor their humanity today? How might you cut them some slack and hold compassion in your heart or extend some compassion to them?

✆ 352 ✆

Letting Go

Some situations or relationships may warrant letting go. Using NVC to the best of your ability to live your values does not necessarily mean that others will respond in the ways you like. Sometimes there is lack of capacity or lack of willingness on the part of another. If you have made your very best effort to connect and to meet needs and have needs met, and the relationship is not meeting your needs and you experience ongoing discomfort, it may be time to let go. This does not mean either person is right or wrong. Using a needs-based mindset will allow you to acknowledge and navigate letting go with respect and care for both of you. Take a look today to see if there is a relationship you are holding onto which fits this description. If you find one, take some time to sit with and write about the feelings and needs that are present for you in this relationship.

∽ 353 ∽
Letting Go

If you are examining a relationship for letting go, take some time today to acknowledge what has been important and meaningful for you in the relationship. What beauty do you find? What struggles can you acknowledge? What have you contributed to the challenges? What do you see the other has contributed to the challenges? How have each of you contributed to the good aspects of the relationship? What are the deal-breakers in terms of unmet needs that lead you to want to let go?

∽ 354 ∽
Letting Go

Continuing the process of letting go, explore what you want to express to this person for some understanding and completion if you were to talk with them about shifting the relationship. You may or may not have this conversation. Explore and write about what you would say if you decided to speak to them. You may want to include some of what you discovered yesterday. Making some honest expressions, including needs and feelings and connection requests, can help with shifting and creating conscious closure. If you want to have a conversation, reach out to the person and invite them to talk.

❧ 355 ❧
Boundaries

Today, take some time to explore what some of your most important needs are in relation to being with other people. What needs are non-negotiables for you in close relationships, in work relationships, with general acquaintances, and needs you would stand up for in community whether you know a person or not? Write a bit about each of these non-negotiable needs and why they are important to you.

❧ 356 ❧
Boundaries

Explore today what comes up in you when someone says or does something that is in opposition to one of your strongly held needs. Here are some things to look at: What do you feel? How do you act? Do you fight, freeze, or flee? Do you stand up for your needs verbally or perhaps physically? How does this sound or look?

❧ 357 ❧
Boundaries Pushed

We all have our limits in terms of how we want to be treated, regarded, or spoken to. Based on needs, what limits are important to you? What kinds of things are unacceptable to you in your interactions or relationships? A few examples include honesty, broken agreements, raised voices, cursing, power struggles, controlling, fighting, physical contact without asking, unresponsiveness, blame and judgment. Notice today if anyone is brushing up against or pushing your limits or crossing your sense of a boundary or has done so in the past. What are the underlying needs? How does this crossing of your boundaries impact you and the relationship?

❧ 358 ❧
Boundaries Upfront

Spend some time writing today about how you can express your limits or non-negotiable needs upfront in a relationship. How can you use NVC to create an honest expression that includes your feelings and needs in a way that holds care for the other person as well? Try writing a few expressions and running them by a trusted friend to see how they land.

❧ 359 ❧
Boundaries Crossed

Imagine you have not expressed your limits around certain needs in a relationship and someone says or does something that crosses over your tolerance level so that you are concerned for your well-being on some level. How might you express with clarity and honesty about this situation to the person? Try writing a few versions of expressions and running them by a trusted friend to get some feedback.

❧ 360 ❧

Essence is Constant

Take some time today to sit quietly. Notice how there is a you that is noticing your experience.

There are thoughts and feelings and beautiful needs. There are sensations. There is a sense of energy and aliveness in you. Notice all of that. Again, notice the one who is noticing. Notice the *you* that is the *I* you think of when you say, "I feel" or "I sense" or "I know" or "I have this need." Notice the consciousness that is this *I*. Notice it is the same I that has been your awareness your whole life. Simply pay attention to this and what it is like. Notice the essence that is the constant aspect that you consider to be you.

❧ 361 ❧

The Nature of Your Essence

Today, notice again the essence of you, the consciousness that is always present and aware. Notice that thoughts and feelings, sensations, needs, experiences, relationships, all come and go. Something remains. Notice this throughout your day as well. Pause frequently and notice your essence, the *you* that is underneath thoughts, feelings and experiences. What is this essence like? What is the nature of *you* at this level? These are some words that capture it for me: space, peace, love, energy, stillness, flow, openness, presence. Your experience of your essence is unique to you. Simply relax and inquire and notice. There is no right or wrong answer. Write or express creatively a bit about your experience of this.

⊰⊱ 362 ⊰⊱
Relax into Essence

Today, put your attention on the nature of your essence as you have discovered it over the past days. Relax as you notice the beauty of your deeper self, the life energy that animates and motivates you. After spending some time sitting in this, gently inquire what movement or expression you would like to engage in today with full awareness and alignment with your essence. Let this deeper essence be your guide in moving into any action.

⊰⊱ 363 ⊰⊱
Look Deeply

You have moved through a year of guided experience. You have practiced many aspects of the consciousness and skills of NVC and written or expressed creatively to integrate your process.

Take some time today to review your year of practice, writing, and expressing. Take note of your journey from where you were when you started to where you are now. Use these prompts to enjoy the impact of your journey. Describe how your sense of self-connection has been impacted. Does your communication with others look different now? If so, in what ways? Has your way of responding to difficult messages shifted? If so, how? How has your confidence in communication been impacted? What impact has this year of focus had on your key relationships?

❧ 364 ❧
Looking Forward

Considering the journey of integration and practice of this year, what areas of your NVC skills and consciousness would you like to continue to strengthen? How would you like to do that? Connect deeply with your essence and your feelings and needs as you consider these questions.

❧ 365 ❧
Gratitude

Today, please take time to acknowledge yourself fully for what you have done over this past year. Spend as much time as you want to enjoy naming the observations of what you have done, how you feel, the needs you have met, the qualities you have embodied, the work you have done! Find a way to celebrate with joy and full expression! Share with someone else about your accomplishment and let them celebrate with you. Give yourself deep appreciation.

Congratulations on completing this exploration guide!

I acknowledge you for your commitment, your passion, and the energy and effort you have given to living your deepest values more fully through integrating NVC! Thank you for adding your unique authenticity and compassion to humanity! Know that you are in good company with all those who are engaging in this work, the work of compassion, connection, healing and awakening. Know that what you have done matters and makes a difference in your world and therefore, our world! Thank you for your participation!

Continue Learning with Kathy

You are warmly invited to participate in live courses as well as on demand courses with Kathy. Individual coaching to address your unique challenges is available by appointment. Visit Kathy's Communication Works website at www.nvctrainingsource.com to contact her.

Kathy's Definitions of Terms

Acknowledgment – Stating awareness and sharing appreciation of people's words and actions that have met needs.

Attachment – A strong desire for something to be a certain way. When we want only a particular strategy or outcome, we struggle to be open to or accept other possible outcomes or strategies. Attachment limits our ability to collaborate and can lead us to suffering when our strategies are not used.

Authenticity – The practice of expressing what is true for you without pretense. Being willing to speak what is in your heart with clarity and self-responsibility.

Beauty of Needs – Noticing the qualities of life we call needs, how they are each unique and contributing to life in profound ways.

Celebration – Acknowledging and enjoying needs that are met. Sharing the observation, feelings, and needs, insights, success, that which gives joy. Allowing the time and space to really enjoy and appreciate the good things that happen, and the needs met.

Collaboration – After sharing and clarifying each person's feelings and needs with care and inclusion, we work together to create strategies we can all agree on to meet the stated needs. With this quality of connection, working together becomes exciting and creative. Follow up and re-evaluation of the strategies supports ongoing collaboration and success.

Compassion – a deep feeling of empathy, warmth, understanding and care for others' or our own experiences and struggles. Often accompanied by a desire to alleviate the pain and suffering.

Congruence – Acting and speaking and physically expressing in alignment with your inner experience, beliefs, and values.

Connection – Understanding one another's feelings and needs with a sense of care and mattering that leads to appreciating how we are together in a particular situation, relationship, or life in general. May include a sense of warm flow, resonance, or even oneness with another person.

Curiosity – The focus of curiosity in NVC is on wondering about what the facts are, what feelings are present, what needs and values are important, and what requests we may desire to make life more wonderful for everyone involved. We do not focus on wondering who is right or wrong, who is to blame, or who deserves punishment and reward. We are curious what is at the heart of the matter.

Empathy – The warm, compassionate, and respectful understanding of someone's experience. Letting a person know they are understood either silently or through reflections of their feelings, needs, and possible requests without judgment. Caring accompaniment with someone who is sharing their experience.

Empowerment – Having the skills, ability, and confidence to make choices and decisions, speak up for them, and access inner and outer resources to meet needs. Doing this with connection to feelings and needs, holding care for the needs of all concerned, while having compassion supports empowerment.

Feelings – emotions and sensations experienced within an individual, stimulated by needs and thoughts. Feelings alert us that something matters to us at the level of needs/values. They are distinct from thoughts and judgments. Feelings are inner experiences.

Honest Expression – speaking what is important to us responsibly by using clear observations, feelings, needs, and requests.

Humanness – the inherent qualities, characteristics, and experiences that define us as human beings. The essence of what it means to be human, embracing our strengths, vulnerabilities, and the potential for growth, connection, and meaningful experiences.

Interdependence – The state in which individuals or groups rely on one another and mutually need one another for support and functioning. The recognition of our interconnectedness and mutual influence and impact. Knowing that our choices and actions have a ripple effect on relationships, systems, and life.

Journal – used as a verb meaning to write or creatively express about experiences, insights, and explorations as you learn and practice NVC. Also used as a noun meaning the place you do your writing and expression about your processes and learning, like a notebook, computer file, art pad, etc.

Living Energy of Needs – The concept that needs each have a unique energy and impact on our bodies, our energy, our emotions and that they exist as life energy we can sense, identify, and call upon because they exist in and of themselves.

Natural giving – One of the underlying assumptions in NVC that states that it is our nature as human beings to want to give to one another and to contribute to life in positive ways.

We access this most readily when we feel we have a choice in the matter.

Needs – Universal qualities of life that are held as values contributing to survival, well-being, satisfaction, and fulfillment, shared by humans as common ground. Meeting needs motivates human behaviors.

Nonviolent Communication - Model of communication developed by Marshall B. Roseberg, PhD, Author of *"Nonviolent Communication, A Language of Life"* Puddledancer Press.

Observation – description of facts that can be seen or heard. The stimulus that is a reference point for the topic of an honest expression.

Pause – Stop conversation when one or more people are stimulated in a conversation and are in a fight, flight, or freeze mode it is hard to communicate responsibly. Creating a pause in the interaction allows people to regulate and do self-empathy to gain calm and clarity before returning to conversation. Letting others know how long of a pause is needed creates trust in coming back to dialogue.

Presence – The essence of consciousness that we are aware of when we are at peace beyond our thinking and feeling. A deep sense of aliveness that is at the core of being that is ultimately creative, wise, and resourceful.

Present – The state of bringing full attention to the moment without distractions or attention to the past or future.

Protective use of force – stopping action when harm may occur by using physical restriction or verbal boundaries, leaving a situation, or asking someone else to leave. This is done without punishment or anger to create safety. Once safe, the option is to dialogue and create understanding if possible.

Reactivity – The words and behaviors used when our nervous system is activated into a survival mode. We are often disconnected from feelings and needs, unable to stay calm and acting from flight, fright, or freeze survival instincts.

Reflecting – Sharing back what we have heard and understood after someone has spoken. We use reflective questions capturing feelings and needs to check our understanding.

Request – asking for behavior, actions, strategies to meet needs without demanding.

- **Connection Request** – Asking for interactions that clarify and deepen understanding of what is being spoken. Asking for a reflection of what has been expressed to check understanding. Asking for a listener to share how it is to hear something.

- **Action Request** – Asking for a specific and doable action to meet the stated needs.

Self-Empathy – Warm, compassionate, respectful understanding of our own experience. Transforming pain or confusion through translating judgments, assumptions, and blame, into feelings and needs. Being present with love and compassion for self and the feelings and needs present. Allowing new curiosity and ideas to naturally arise after gaining clarity and peace.

Self-Responsibility – recognizing and acknowledging choice and speaking from clarity of observations, feelings, needs, and requests. Understanding the ways we contribute to how situations, interactions and relationships function and how our words and actions impact others.

Sensations – physical, bodily experiences sensed by an individual.

Strategies – plans, actions, and behaviors used to meet universal needs and values.

Triggering – The activation of the nervous system into a flight, fright, or freeze reaction. May be stimulated by words and actions that touch our pain, sense of safety, survival, belonging, respect, mattering, or other unmet needs from the past or present. Emotions may also be stimulated as these needs are touched.

Victim thoughts – Thoughts that indicate a belief that we don't have a choice. These are often words that are intended to share feelings but are interpretations of people's behaviors. (Examples: abandoned, betrayed, intimidated, manipulated, neglected, tricked, smothered.)

Appendix

Emotions When Needs are Met

Absorbed
Adventurous
Affectionate
Alert
Alive
Amazed
Amused
Animated
Anxious
Appreciative
Ardent
Aroused
Astonished
Awed
Bashful
Blissful
Buoyant
Brave
Breathless
Calm
Carefree

Centered
Certain
Cheerful
Comfortable
Compassionate
Complacent
Composed
Concerned
Confident
Content
Cool
Curious
Dazed
Dazzled
Delighted
Determined
Eager
Ecstatic
Effervescent
Elated
Electrified

Empathic
Encouraged
Energetic
Engrossed
Enlivened
Enthusiastic
Exalted
Excited
Exhilarated
Expansive
Expectant
Exuberant
Fascinated
Friendly
Fulfilled
Gay
Genial
Giddy
Glad
Gleeful
Glorious

Glowing
Good-humored
Gracious
Grateful
Gratified
Groovy
Happy
Helpful
Hopeful
Inquisitive
Inspired
Intense
Interested
Intrigued
Invigorated
Involved
Joyful
Joyous
Jubilant
Kind
Keen

Light-hearted
Lively
Longing
Loving
Mellow
Merry
Mirthful
Moved
Open
Optimistic
Overjoyed
Overwhelmed
Passionate
Peaceful
Pensive
Pleased
Proud
Radiant
Rapturous
Refreshed
Relieved

Satisfied
Secure
Sensitive
Serene
Soft
Stimulated
Surprised
Sympathetic
Tender
Thankful
Thoughtful
Thrilled
Tickled
Touched
Tranquil
Trusting
Warm
Zealous
Zippy

Emotions When Needs are Unmet

Aggravated

Agitated

Alarmed

Alienated

Aloof

Angry

Anguished

Annoyed

Antagonistic

Antsy

Anxious

Apathetic

Appalled

Apprehensive

Aroused

Ashamed

Aversive

Bewildered

Bitter

Blah

Blue

Brokenhearted

Careful

Cautious

Chagrined

Cold

Concerned

Confounded

Confused

Contrite

Cool

Cranky

Credulous

Crestfallen

Cross

Curious

Dejected

Depressed

Despairing

Despondent

Desperate

Detached

Disappointed

Disconnected

Discouraged

Disheartened

Disgruntled

Disgusted

Disinterested

Dismayed

Disoriented

Dispirited

Disquieted

Distressed

Down

Dread

Disturbed

Downcast

Downhearted

Dull

Edgy

Embarrassed

Embittered

Empty

Enraged

Envious

Exasperated

Exhausted

Fatigued

Fearful

Fidgety

Flustered

Foggy

Forlorn

Fretful

Frightened

Frustrated

Funky

Furious

Gloomy

Glum

Grief

Grouchy

Hateful

Heartbroken

Helpless

Hesitant

Horrified
Hostile
Hurt
Impatient
Indifferent
Inert
Infuriated
Insecure
Irate
Irked
Irritated
Jealous
Jittery
Jumpy
Lazy
Lethargic
Listless
Lonely
Longing
Low
Mad
Mean
Melancholic
Miffed
Miserable
Mopey
Morose

Mystified
Nervous
Nettled
Numb
Overexcited
Overwhelmed
Panicky
Pain/ed
Paralyzed
Peeved
Perplexed
Pressure
Puzzled
Rancorous
Regretful
Repugnance
Repulsion
Resentful
Restless
Reluctant
Sad
Scared
Sensitive
Sensuous
Shaky
Sheepish
Shock/ed

Skeptical
Somber
Sorrowful
Sour
Speechless
Spiteful
Startled
Subdued
Sullen
Surprised
Surly
Suspicious
Tender
Tenuous
Ticked off
Terrified
Terror
Ticked off
Timid
Tired
Trepidation
Troubled
Uncertain
Uncomfortable
Uneasy
Unhappy
Unnerved

Unsettled	Vengeful	Withdrawn
Unsure	Vexed	Woeful
Upset	Vindictive	Worried
Unsteady	Weak	Wretched
Uptight	Weepy	Yearning

Adapted from Susan Skye

Body Sensations

Quality of Movement	Well-being or vitality	Nerve Quality
Shaky	Grounded	Prickly
Sensitive	Balanced	Tingling
Tender	Relaxed	Pulsing
Achy	Open	Electric
Bruised	Calm	Twitchy
Nauseous	Loose	Radiating
Fluttery	Light	Burning
Pounding	Soft	Buzzy
Throbbing	Springy	Vibrating
Trembly	Mushy	Sharp
Dizzy	Spacious	Stabbing
Spacey	Energized	Intense
Lightheaded	Smooth	Pain
Breathless	Airy	Racing
Queasy	Flowing	Achy
Wobbly	Expanded	Searing
Bubbly	Expansive	Burning
		Rough
		Smooth
		Gliding

Temperature Related	Constriction/ Low Energy	Thick
Warm	Constricted	Heavy
Hot	Compressed	Dense
Sweaty	Congested	Sticky
Burning	Blocked	Stiff
Clammy	Depleted	Knotted
Cool	Clenched	Hollow
Cold	Closed	Empty
Chilly	Depleted	Tired
Frozen	Numb	Exhausted
Shivering	Hard	Rigid
Dripping	Tense	Floating
	Tight	Full
		Tingly

Universal Human Needs/Values

A basic list of qualities that sustain us.

Autonomy
Autonomy
Choice
Freedom
Independence
Space
Spontaneity
Flexibility

Connection
Acceptance
Affection
Appreciation
Belonging
Care
Closeness
Communication
Community
Companionship
Compassion
Consideration
Consistency
Cooperation
Dependability
Empathy
Inclusion
Intimacy

Love
Mutuality
Nurturing
Reliability
Respect/self-respect
Safety
Security
Stability
Serving
Support
To know and be known
To see and be seen
To be understood
To be heard
Trust
Warmth
Understanding

Honesty
Authenticity
Integrity
Openness
Presence
Congruence
Truth
Vulnerability

Play
Joy
Humor
Fun

Peace
Beauty
Communion
Ease
Equality
Equanimity
Harmony
Calm
Inspiration
Order
Space

Well-Being
Air
Comfort
Food
Health
Energy
Movement/exercise
Nourishment
Nurture
Order

Live Compassion

Predictability	**Meaning**	Growth
Rest/sleep	Awareness	Hope
Sexual expression	Celebration of life	Inspiration
Safety	Challenge	Learning
Shelter	Clarity	Mourning
Stability	Competence	Participation
Sustainability	Consciousness	Presence
Touch	Contribution	Purpose
Water	Creativity	Self-expression
Warmth	Discovery	Stimulation
	Efficacy	To matter
	Effectiveness	

Adapted from Marshall B. Rosenberg, PhD

Testimonials

"I'm a better person for having been through this program. I appreciate how it has helped me redefine success. NVC is a way of life and I recognize that I will never be perfect, but I can try to do better from one moment to the next. It has shifted the way I think about myself and my interactions with others. I have a set of tools and practices to use to enhance my life. It has become a lighthouse that guides my journey. It has also given me hope for a better future for the human race." *Denise Liebetrau, HR & Compensation Consultant, Prosper Consulting*

"NVC has helped me tremendously in my life and in particular in communicating in relationships. I am a much better listener and communicator. Kathy's classes are very convenient for developing deeper and stronger NVC skills. I use a number of the NVC practices on a daily basis to stay positive and in harmony. Kathy is very sensitive in her responses to her students and skillful as a teacher. I generally feel very clear and empowered by the end of each class." *Vic Weese*

"If serving others is your passion and brings you great joy, compassionate communication is a practice that will allow you to tap even deeper into that spirit of connectedness inside you." *Tiffany Maurycy, Orion Advisor*

"NVC has helped with giving administrators/supervisors skills to have difficult conversations. I have found these leaders are less avoidant of these hard conversations and feel better prepared to have these conversations in a way that is honoring and respectful. Overall, NVC has increased our agency's ability to engage in respectful and empathic dialogue with each other, with staff and with our clients." *Lori Oswald, Human Services Director*

"Kathy has a gift of presence that brings us home to "the heart of the matter" within ourselves and with our community. It is important to have passion and love for what we want to offer, but it is really an art to make that passion into a deliverable and palatable message to the world. Kathy does that." *Maria Bailey, Integral Coach and Facilitator and Zen Priest*

"Kathy does an amazing job of making the materials clear, accessible and something that can be put into use in our everyday lives. I highly recommend her trainings and workshops" *Lisa Stokes Nicholas, Kavi Consulting Services*

"I am grateful for the safe and supportive space Kathy made for me to explore my feelings and needs and arrive at new understanding and appreciation for myself. Through the acceptance of Kathy and our group I regained access to hope, trust, and my innocence. I can finally feel a connection between my head and my heart and taste real compassion for myself and others. It is a place of rich, deep peace and possibility. I can't say "Thank you!" enough. Kathy's skill in teaching, living, and modeling NVC is inspiring. She makes it look so easy, because she stays grounded in Presence, able to trust the unfolding of wisdom through the process of NVC. I could not have asked for any finer teacher to show the way to Compassionate

Communication and connection with self and others!" *Ann Gibson, Immersion Program Graduate*

"Kathy Ziola has a wonderful gift for making this valuable and important process of Compassionate Communication easily accessible to all who attend her workshops. Her excitement and enthusiasm are contagious and energizing." *Tom A, Radio Programmer*

"NVC has had a significant impact on my practice and our organization. As a supervisor NVC has helped me to quell reactivity, listen deeply and have courageous conversations in a meaningful way. The tools are tremendously helpful and something very tangible that I have found myself utilizing on many occasions to prepare for difficult conversations or find some self-compassion or compassion for others when I am upset. I have found that my staff has become more and more responsive to it, as I have become more comfortable using it, which in turn has allowed me to use it in an authentic and genuine way. It does require a great deal of commitment and practice and I believe that it is a practice that is worth it. I have found a deeper understanding, compassion and comfortableness with disagreement. If I had to pick one line to describe the impact it would be; that the weight of trying to win or be right has been lifted from my shoulders and I find my needs and the needs of those around me are being more regularly met and understood creating a more harmonious environment both internally and externally." *Nicki Watson, Supervisor, Adult & Child Protective Services*

About Kathy Ziola

Kathy Ziola is passionate about authenticity, living with presence and compassion, and helping others do the same. Nonviolent Communication has been her path of learning and teaching since 2005. As a certified trainer with the Center for Nonviolent Communication, she has been facilitating training, trainer training, and coaching in a wide variety of settings transforming lives and relationships with compassion and laser sharp insight.

Highlights of her development include a BS degree in Human Development and Family Studies and an MA in Agency Counseling, certifications in massage therapy, yoga, and meditation instruction, and as a Reiki master teacher. Early in her career she organized relationships training events and began teaching and bringing her passion for continuing education into expression. Years of breath work and spiritual inquiry contributed to personal healing and awakening experiences that are the foundation of her ability to support others in healing and growing. Writing poetry has been a lovely companion expression through the years and Kathy often shares her original works in her workshops to add inspiration and humor.

Kathy's thirty-five plus years as a psychotherapist, group facilitator, and healing arts professional have given her deep experience and understanding of our shared humanity and interpersonal relating. Her integration of NVC and development of presence through this work provide a bright clarity that supports readers and students in shifting out of unskilled habits of communication into a new and powerful way of perceiving, being, and expressing fully in life.

While she has enjoyed travel, Kathy has lived most of her life in Colorado where she raised two daughters, loving and sharing in the great outdoors. She enjoys playing and performing improv, hiking, biking, camping and cross-country skiing. Nature nourishes her and rejuvenates her being. Spending time in it helps her sustain balance and health with joy and fun.

Work with Kathy

You are warmly invited to participate in live or on demand courses with Kathy. Private Coaching for your unique challenges is available by appointment. For details, registration and to contact Kathy please visit Kathy's Communication Works Website at nvctrainingsource.com.